HAL•LEONARD®

GUITAR PLAY-ALONG

AUDIO ACCESS INCLUDED

VOL. 99

ZZ TOP

To access audio visit:
www.halleonard.com/mylibrary

Enter Code
1408-9774-1957-6156

Photographed at the 2008 Harley Davidson Celebration, Milwaukee, Wisconsin.

ISBN 978-1-4234-4317-9

7777 W. BLUEMOUND RD. P.O. BOX 13819 MILWAUKEE, WI 53213

In Australia Contact:
Hal Leonard Australia Pty. Ltd.
4 Lentara Court
Cheltenham, Victoria, 3192 Australia
Email: ausadmin@halleonard.com.au

Visit Hal Leonard Online at
www.halleonard.com

Guitar Notation Legend

THE MUSICAL STAFF shows pitches and rhythms and is divided by bar lines into measures. Pitches are named after the first seven letters of the alphabet.

TABLATURE graphically represents the guitar fingerboard. Each horizontal line represents a string, and each number represents a fret.

Notes: E F C D A B F G E

Strings: high E B G D A low E

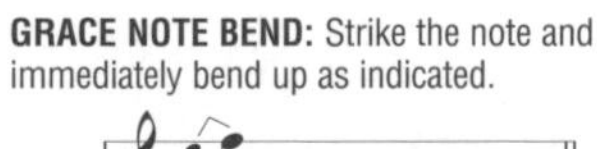

4th string, 2nd fret — 1st & 2nd strings open, played together — open D chord

HALF-STEP BEND: Strike the note and bend up 1/2 step.

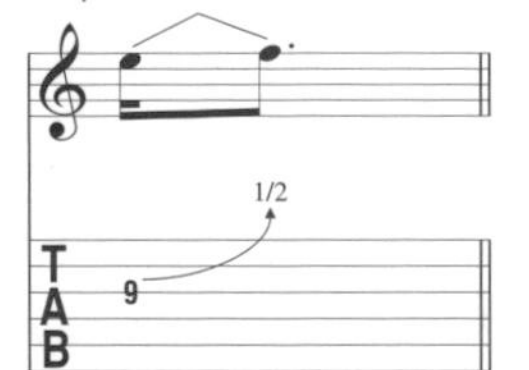

WHOLE-STEP BEND: Strike the note and bend up one step.

GRACE NOTE BEND: Strike the note and immediately bend up as indicated.

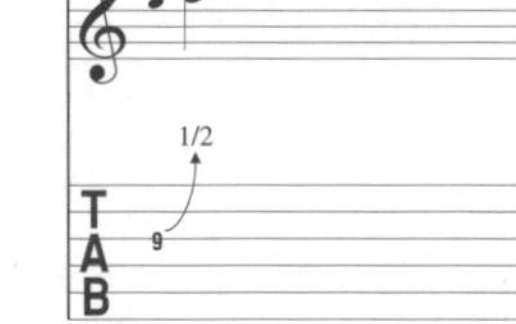

SLIGHT (MICROTONE) BEND: Strike the note and bend up 1/4 step.

BEND AND RELEASE: Strike the note and bend up as indicated, then release back to the original note. Only the first note is struck.

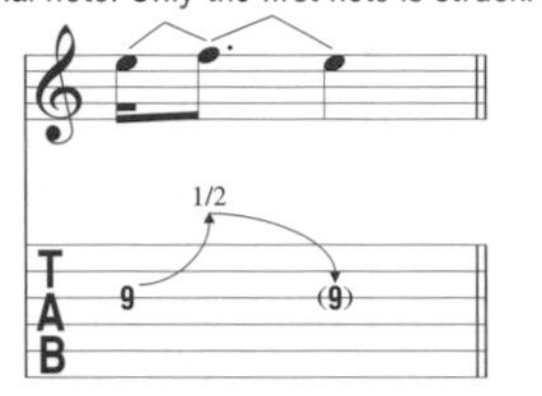

PRE-BEND: Bend the note as indicated, then strike it.

VIBRATO: The string is vibrated by rapidly bending and releasing the note with the fretting hand.

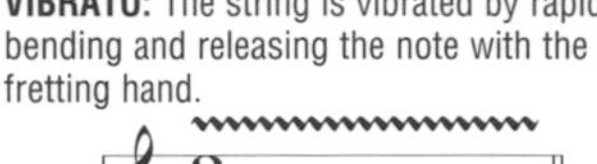

PALM MUTING: The note is partially muted by the pick hand lightly touching the string(s) just before the bridge.

HAMMER-ON: Strike the first (lower) note with one finger, then sound the higher note (on the same string) with another finger by fretting it without picking.

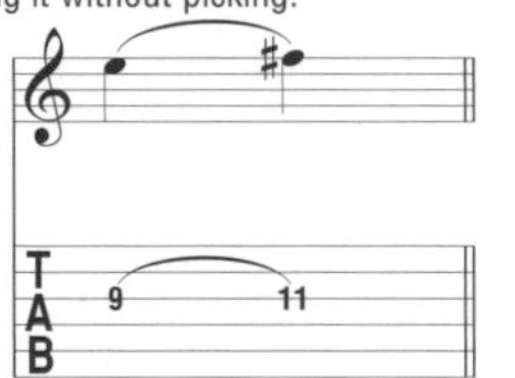

PULL-OFF: Place both fingers on the notes to be sounded. Strike the first note and without picking, pull the finger off to sound the second (lower) note.

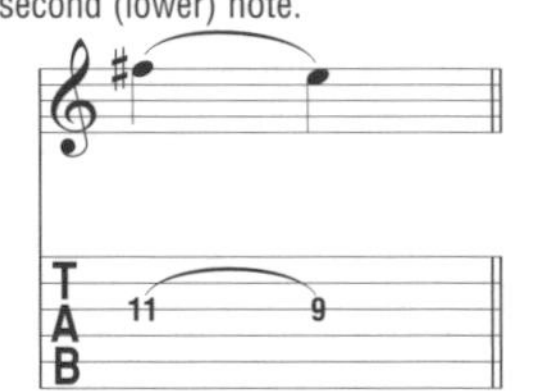

LEGATO SLIDE: Strike the first note and then slide the same fret-hand finger up or down to the second note. The second note is not struck.

SHIFT SLIDE: Same as legato slide, except the second note is struck.

TRILL: Very rapidly alternate between the notes indicated by continuously hammering on and pulling off.

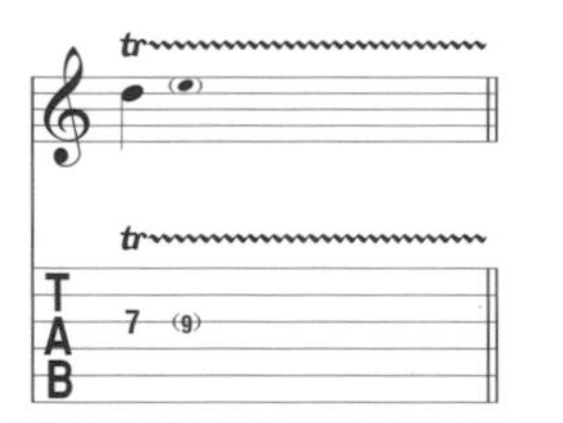

TAPPING: Hammer ("tap") the fret indicated with the pick-hand index or middle finger and pull off to the note fretted by the fret hand.

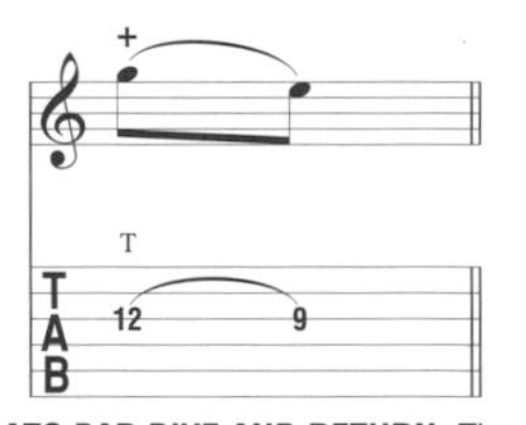

NATURAL HARMONIC: Strike the note while the fret-hand lightly touches the string directly over the fret indicated.

PINCH HARMONIC: The note is fretted normally and a harmonic is produced by adding the edge of the thumb or the tip of the index finger of the pick hand to the normal pick attack.

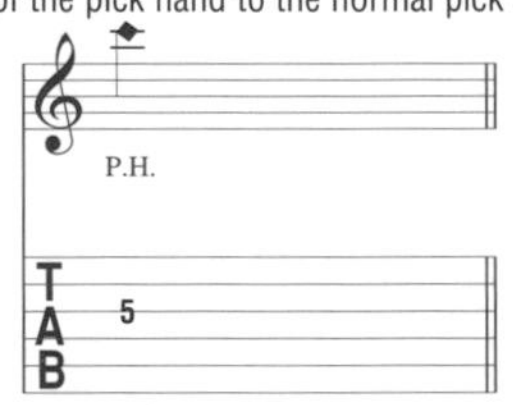

TREMOLO PICKING: The note is picked as rapidly and continuously as possible.

VIBRATO BAR DIVE AND RETURN: The pitch of the note or chord is dropped a specified number of steps (in rhythm), then returned to the original pitch.

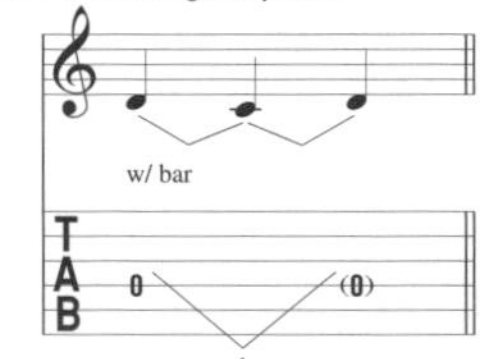

VIBRATO BAR SCOOP: Depress the bar just before striking the note, then quickly release the bar.

VIBRATO BAR DIP: Strike the note and then immediately drop a specified number of steps, then release back to the original pitch.

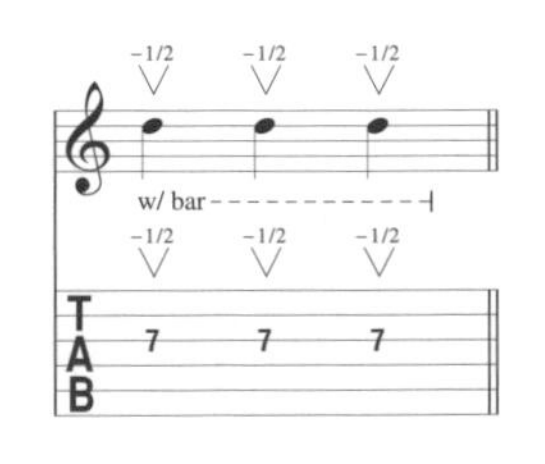

Additional Musical Definitions

(accent) • Accentuate note (play it louder).

(staccato) • Play the note short.

D.S. al Coda • Go back to the sign (𝄋), then play until the measure marked "***To Coda***," then skip to the section labelled "**Coda.**"

D.C. al Fine • Go back to the beginning of the song and play until the measure marked "***Fine***" (end).

Fill • Label used to identify a brief melodic figure which is to be inserted into the arrangement.

N.C. • Harmony is implied.

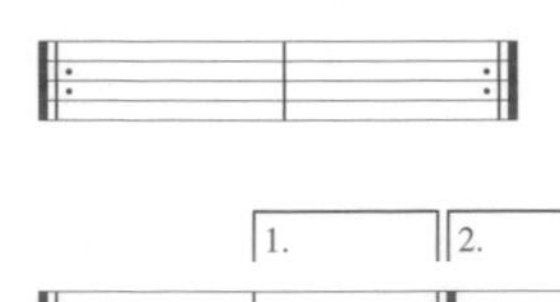

• Repeat measures between signs.

• When a repeated section has different endings, play the first ending only the first time and the second ending only the second time.

HAL•LEONARD®

GUITAR PLAY-ALONG

AUDIO ACCESS INCLUDED

VOL. 99

CONTENTS

Cheap Sunglasses

Words and Music by Billy F Gibbons, Dusty Hill and Frank Lee Beard

Gm7 B♭6 C5 Gm7 B♭6 C5
first thing you do when you get up out of bed is
Gm7 B♭6 C5 Gm7 B♭6 C5
hit that street a run - in' and try to beat the mass - es and
Gm7 N.C. G5 F6 G5 B♭6 C5 B♭6
go get your - self some cheap sun - glass - es. Oh,
G5 F6 G5 B♭6 C5 B♭6 G5 F6 G5 B♭6 C5 B♭6
yeah. Oh, yeah. Oh,

To Coda 𝄌

Interlude

G5 F6 G5 F E

Play 4 times

yeah.

w/ clean tone

Guitar Solo

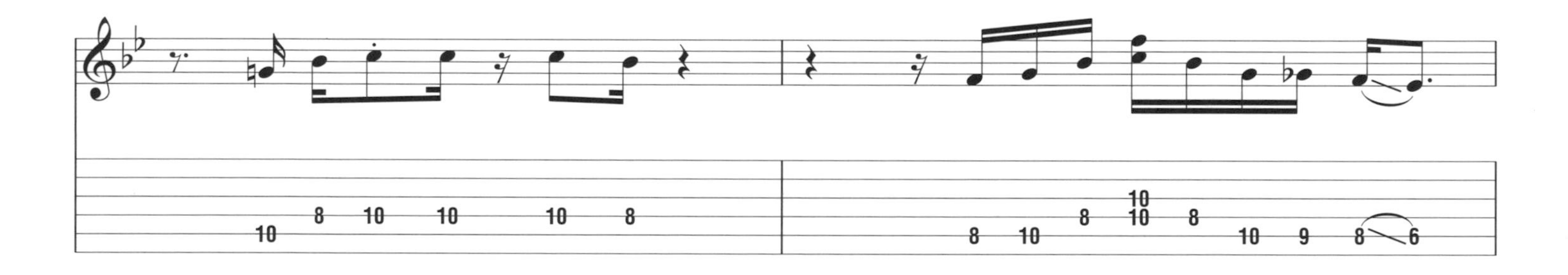

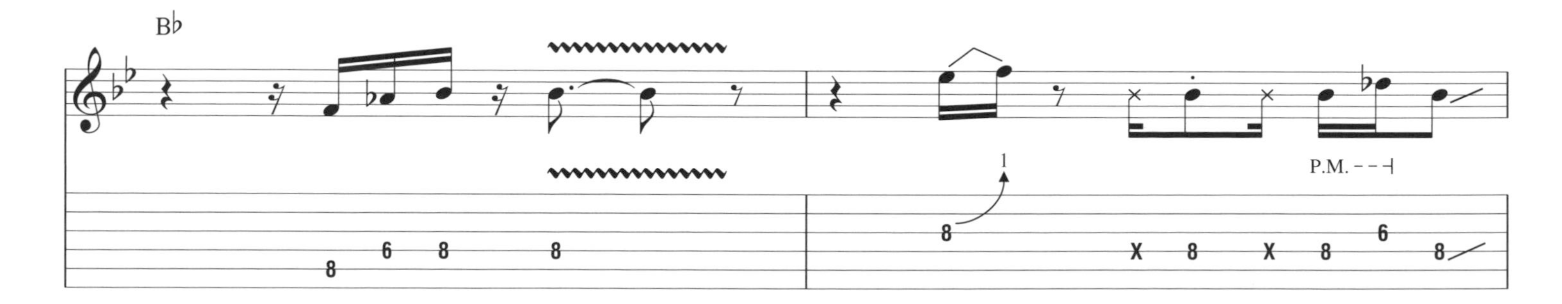

Cm7

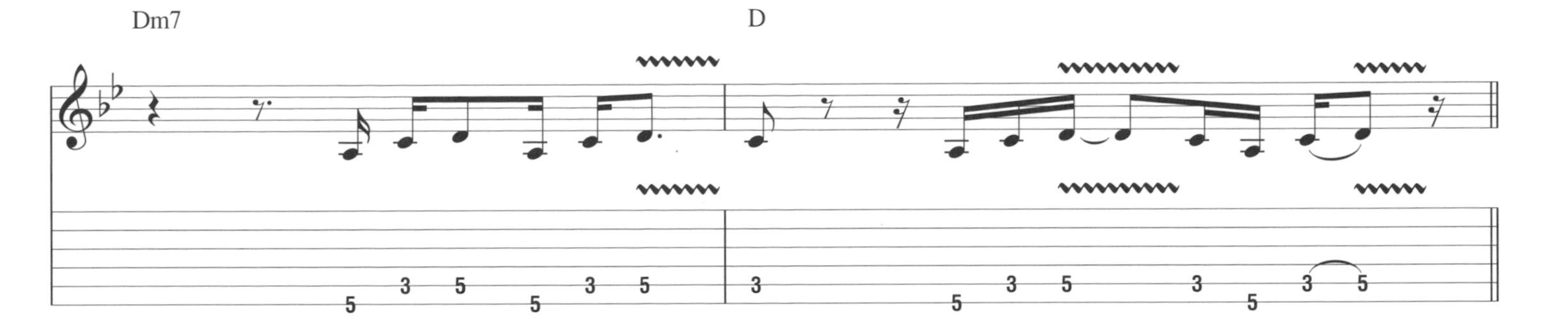
Dm7
D

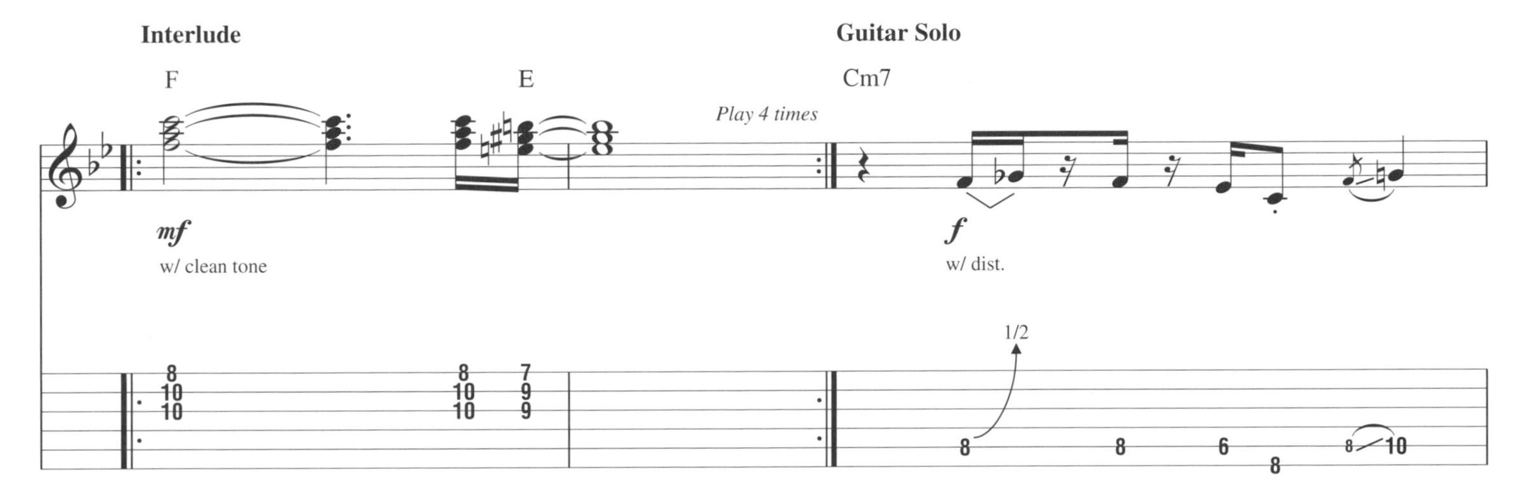
Interlude
Guitar Solo
F
E
Cm7
Play 4 times
mf
w/ clean tone
f
w/ dist.
1/2

P.M.
P.H.

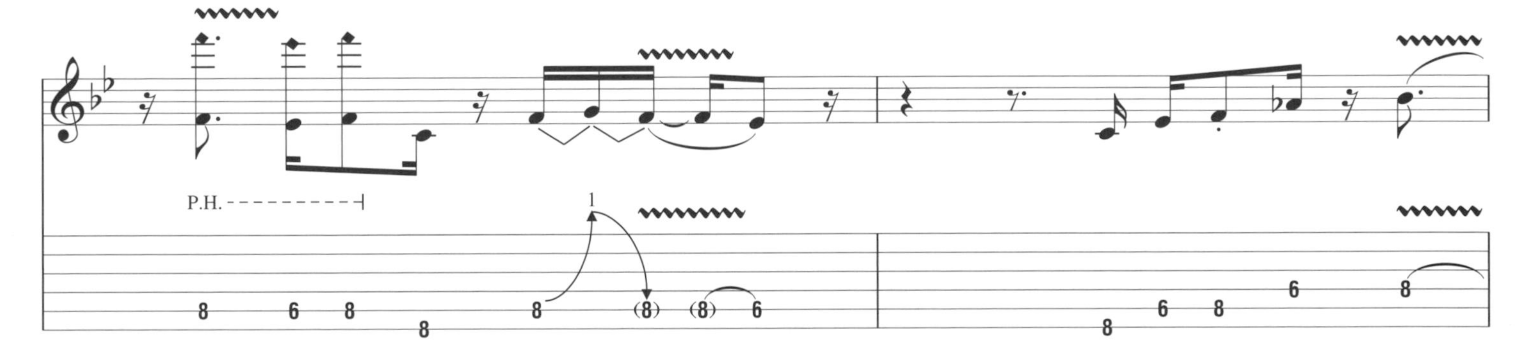
B♭
P.H.
1

Cm7

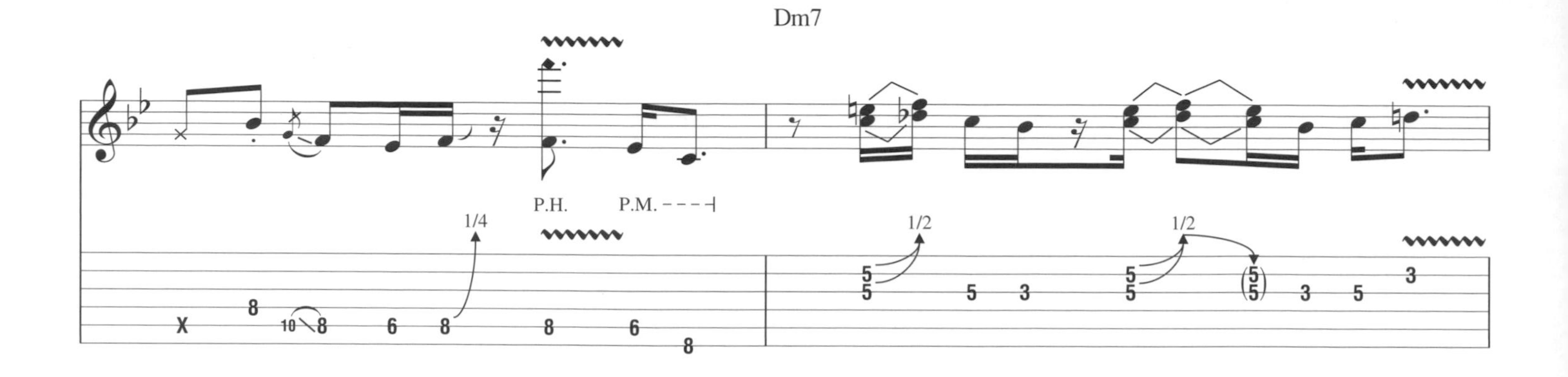
Dm7
P.H.
P.M.
1/4
1/2
1/2

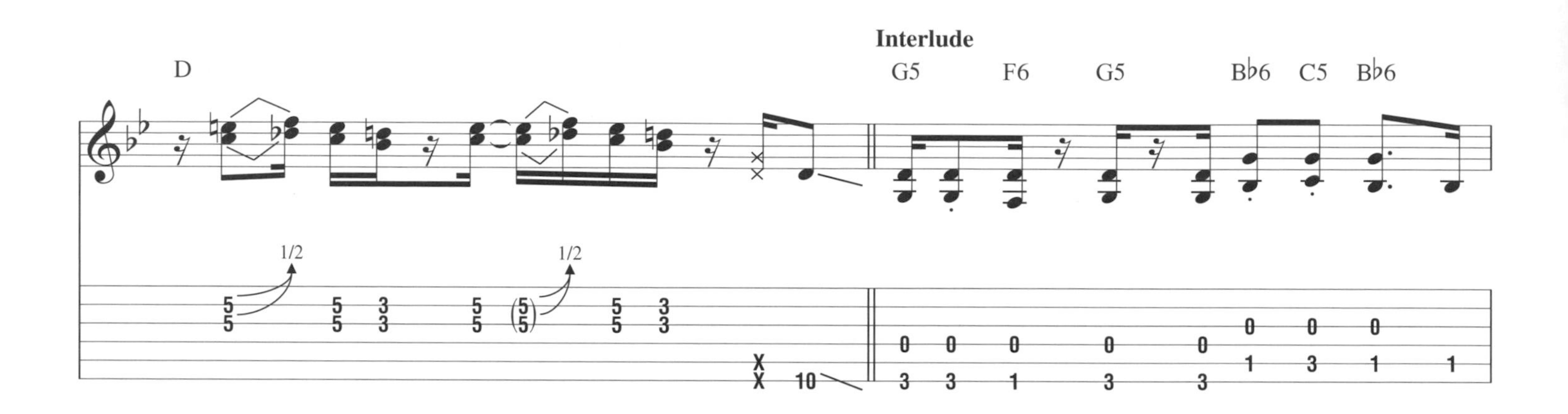
Interlude
D
G5
F6
G5
B♭6
C5
B♭6
1/2
1/2

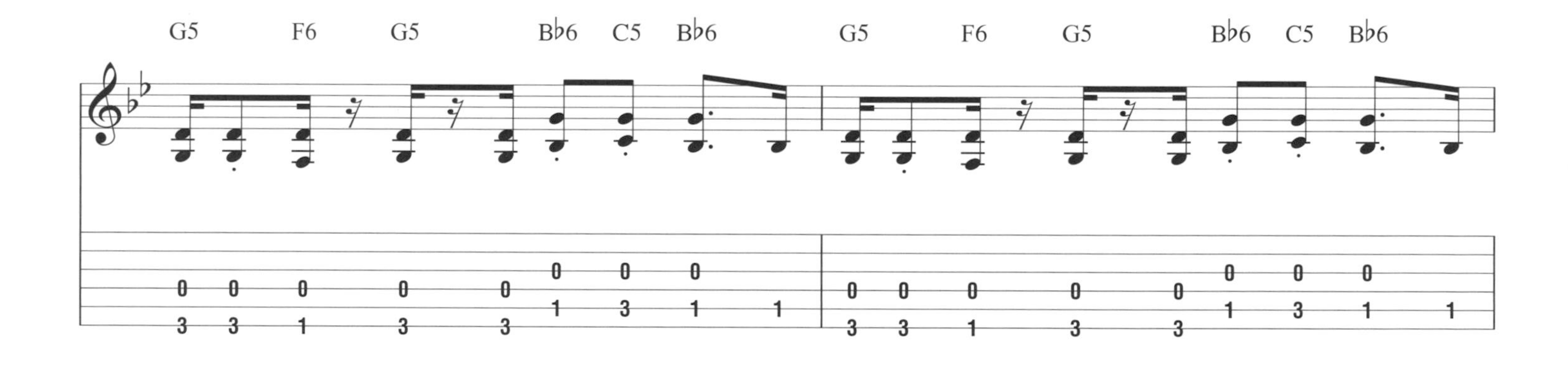
G5
F6
G5
B♭6
C5
B♭6
G5
F6
G5
B♭6
C5
B♭6

D.C. al Coda
G5
F6
G5

Coda

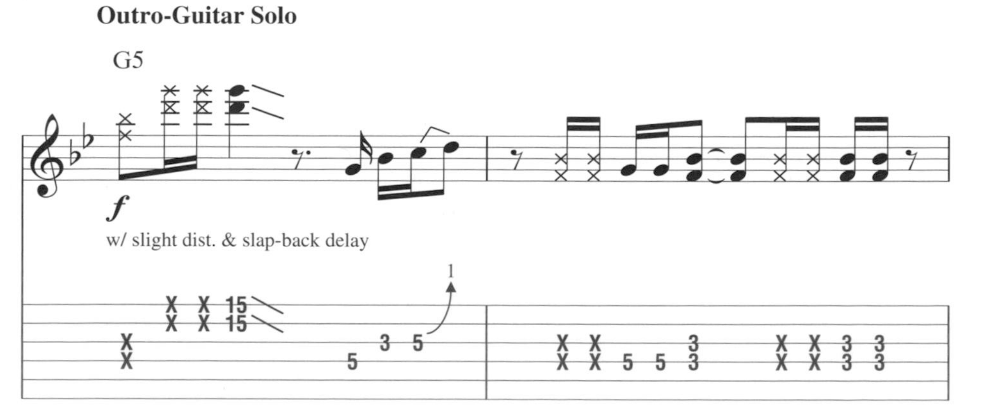
Outro-Guitar Solo
G5
f
w/ slight dist. & slap-back delay
1

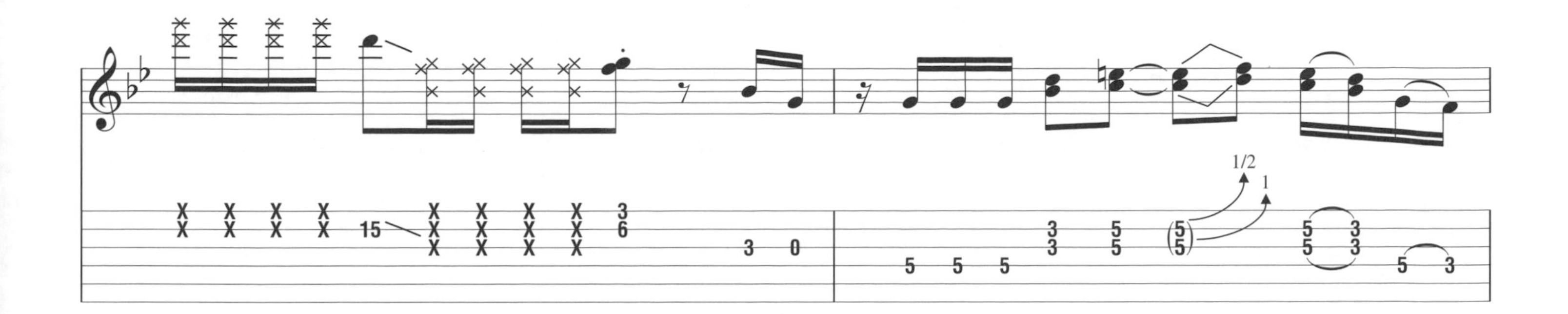
1/2
1

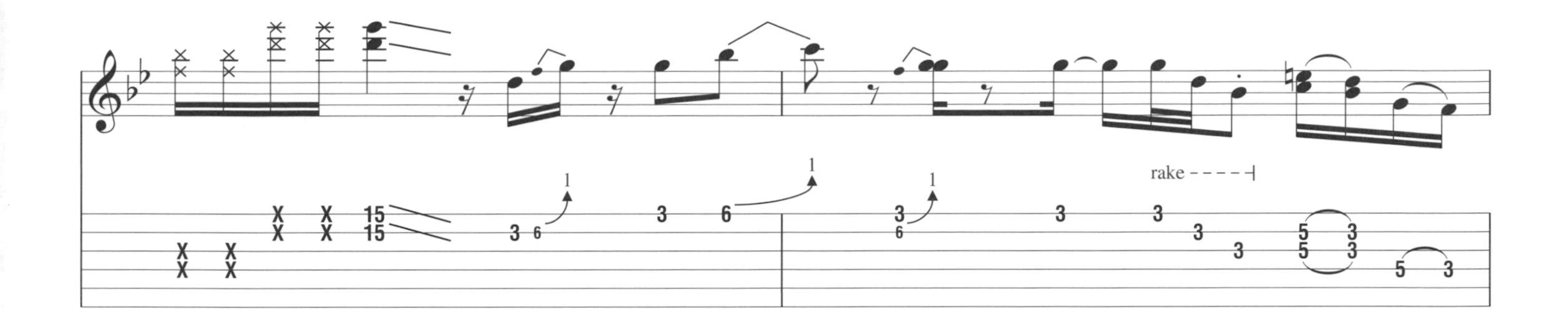
1
1
1
rake

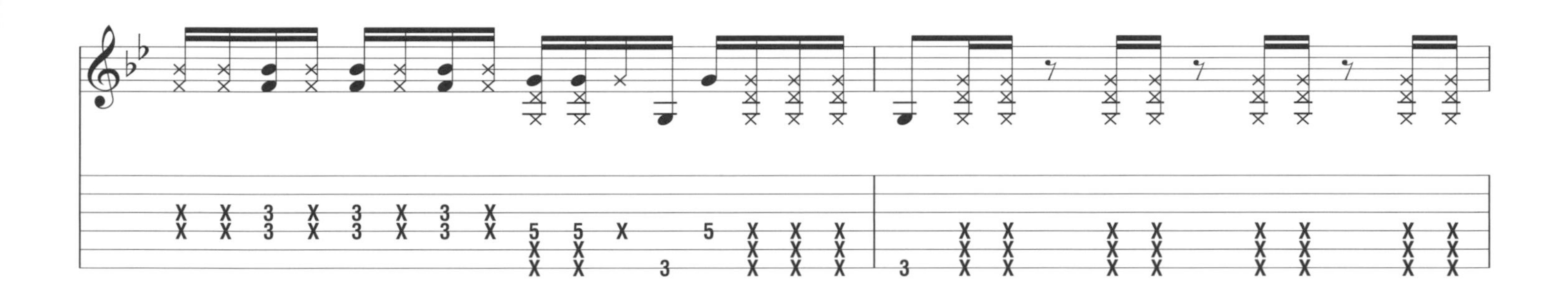

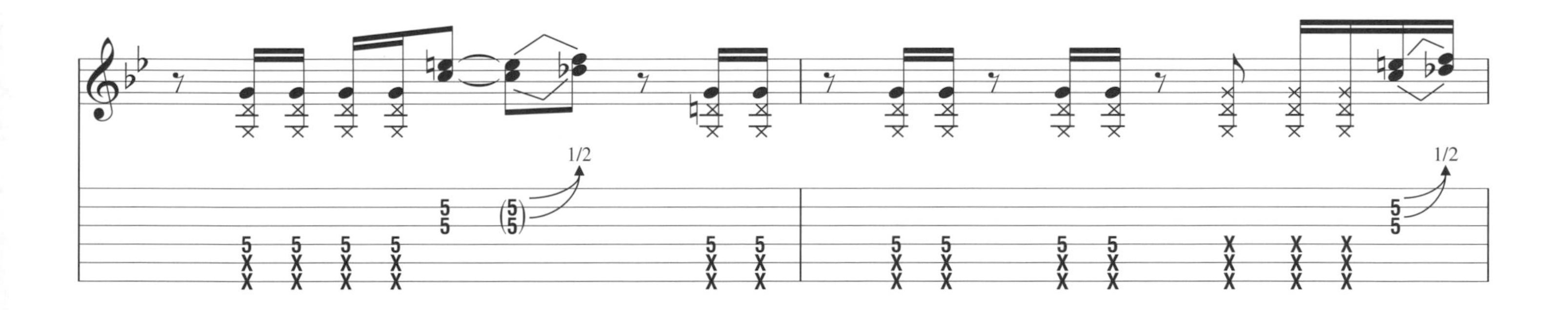
1/2
1/2

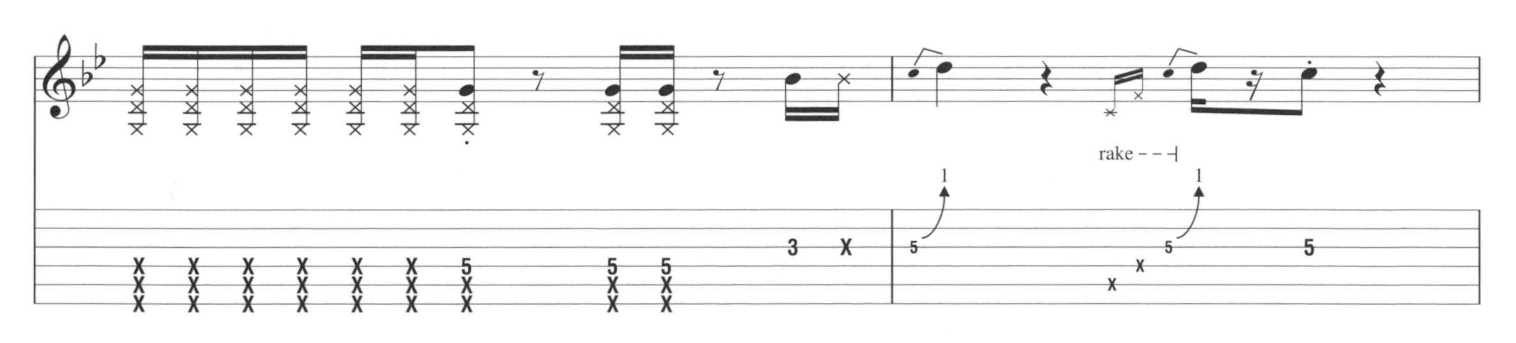
rake
1
1

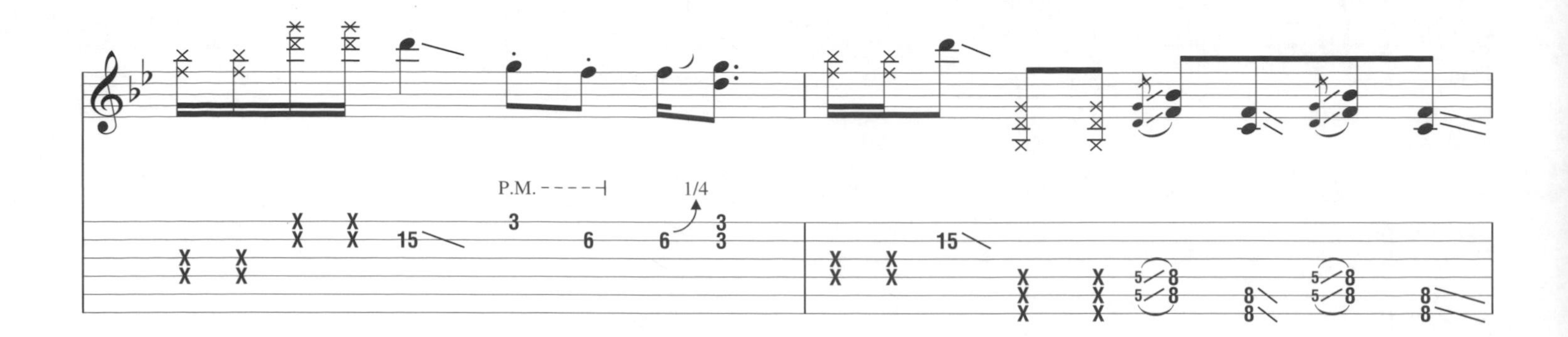
P.M.
1/4

1
1

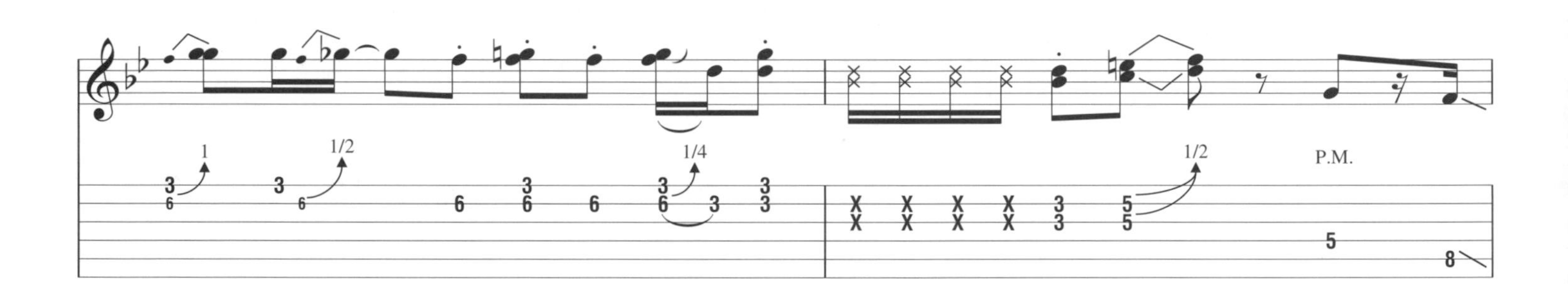
1
1/2
1/4
1/2
P.M.

1
1
1

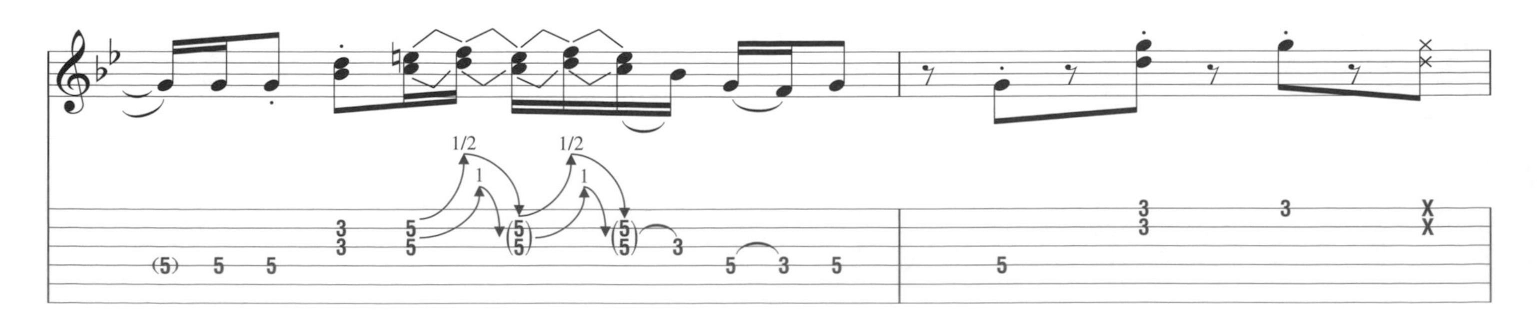
1/2
1
1/2
1

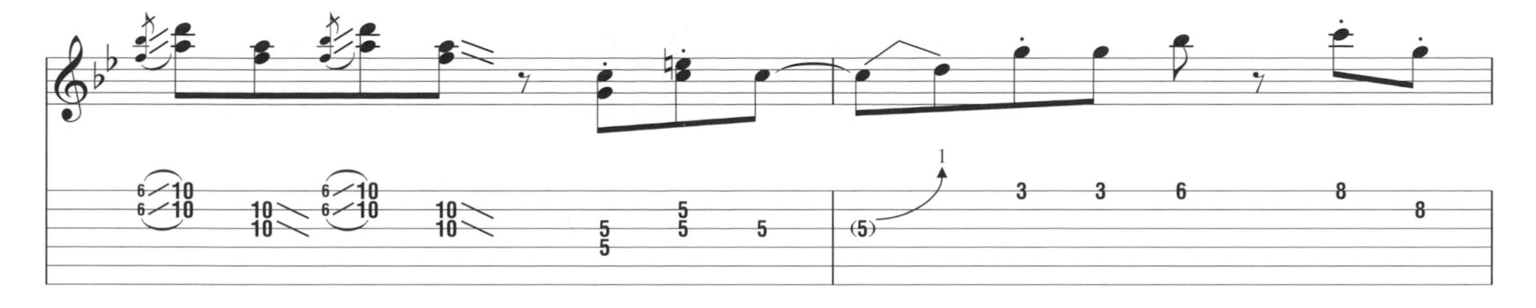

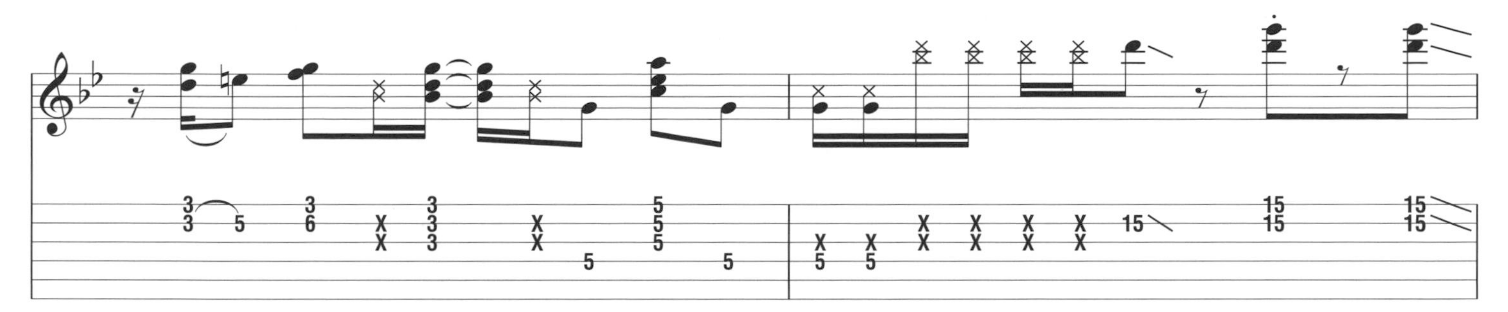

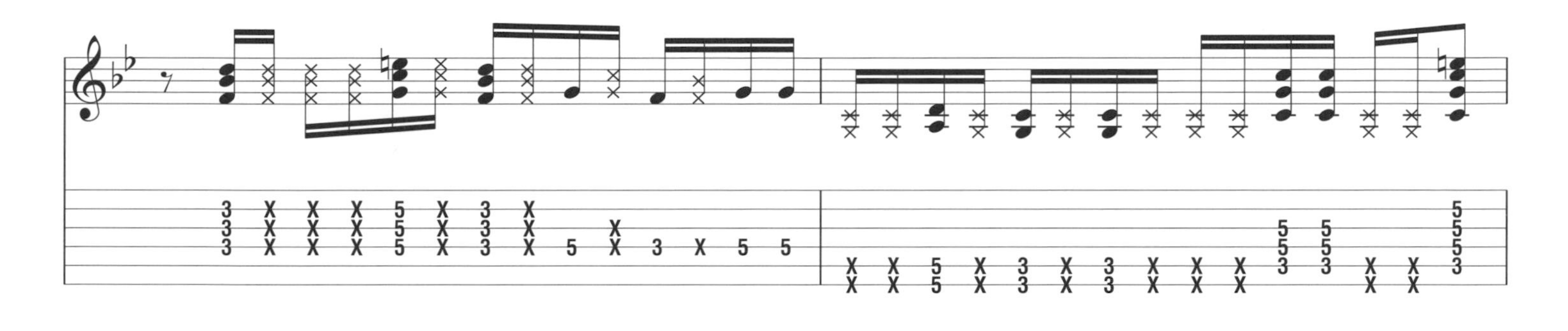

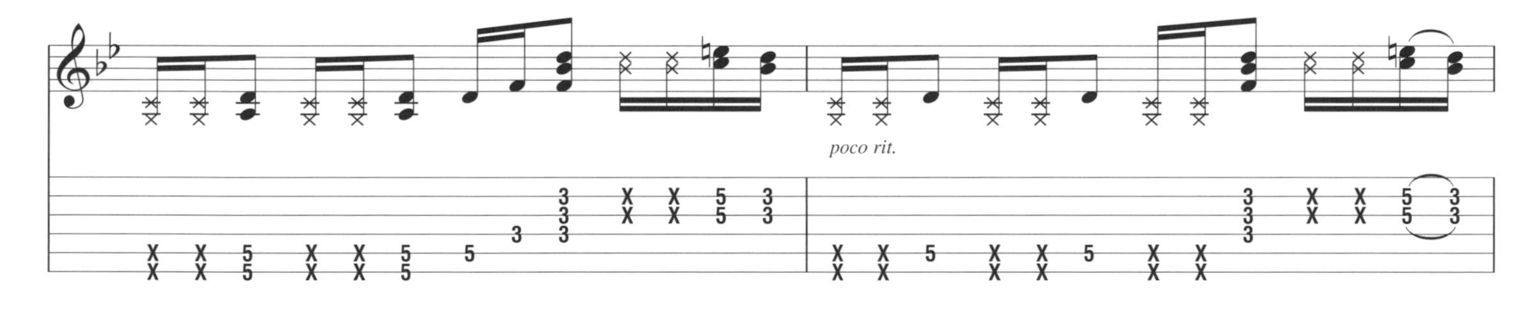

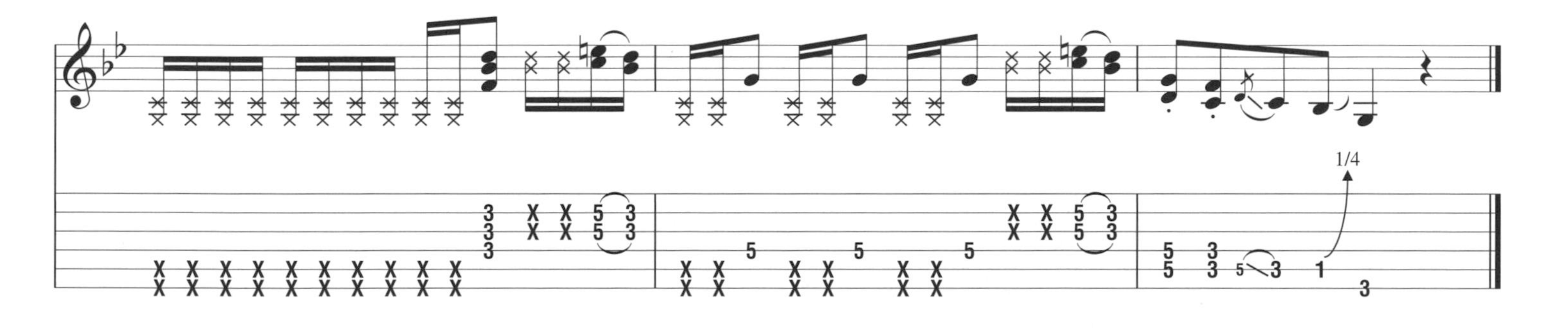

Additional Lyrics

2. Spied a little thing and I followed her all night.
   In her funky fine Levi's and her sweater kinda tight.
   She had a West Coast strut that was sweet as molasses.
   Now, what really knocked me out was her cheap sunglasses.

3. Now, go out and get yourself some thick black frames,
   With the glass so dark they won't even know your name.
   And the choice is up to you 'cause they come in two classes.
   Rhinestone shades or cheap sunglasses.

La Grange

Words and Music by Billy F Gibbons, Dusty Hill and Frank Beard

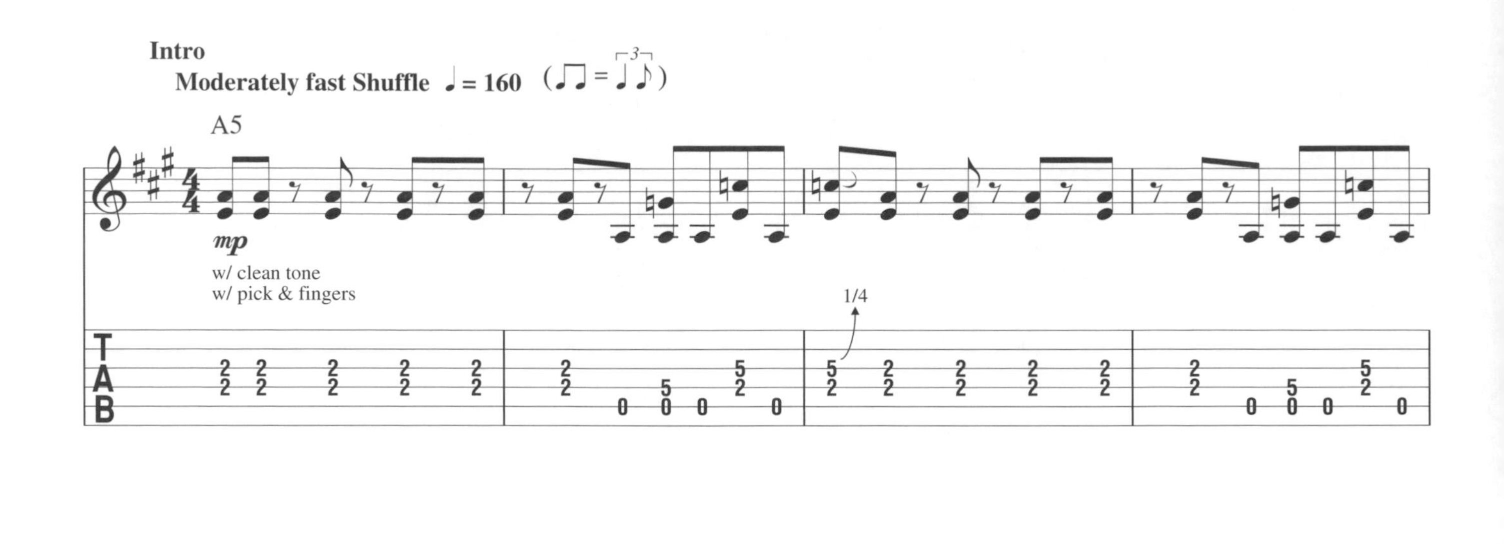

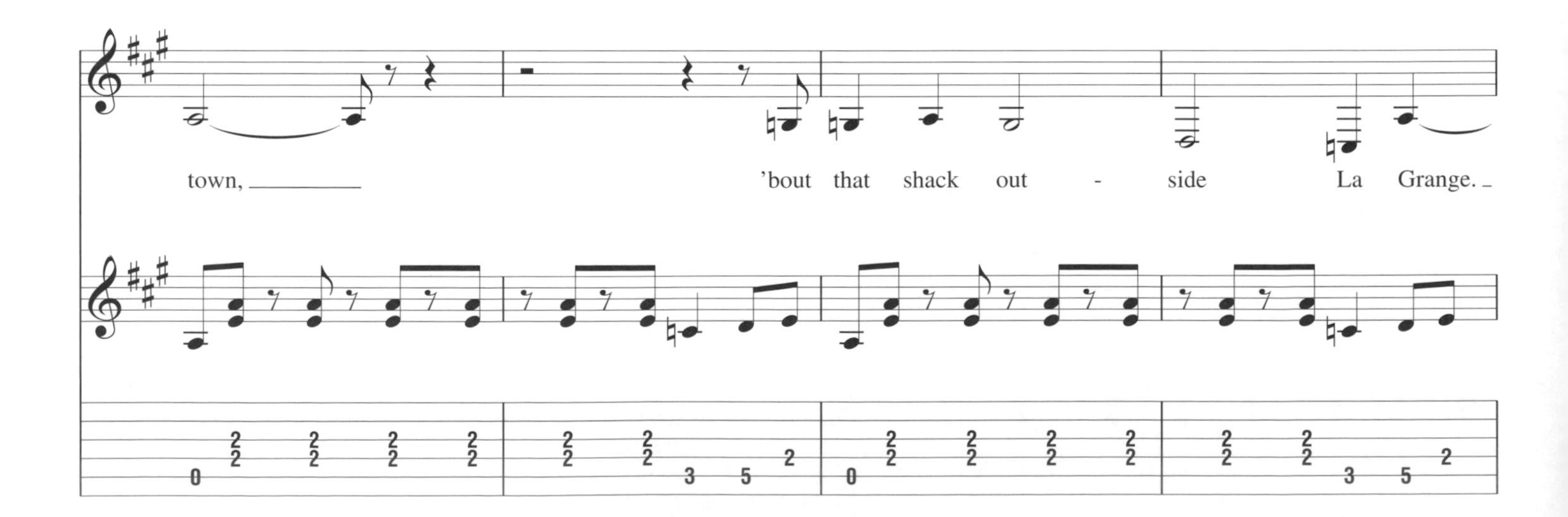

Spoken: And you know what I'm talk-in' a-bout. Just let me know

if you wan-na go to that

home out on the range. Spoken: They got-ta lot-ta nice girls.

N.C.
A5
C5 D5
Have mer - cy.
w/ dist.

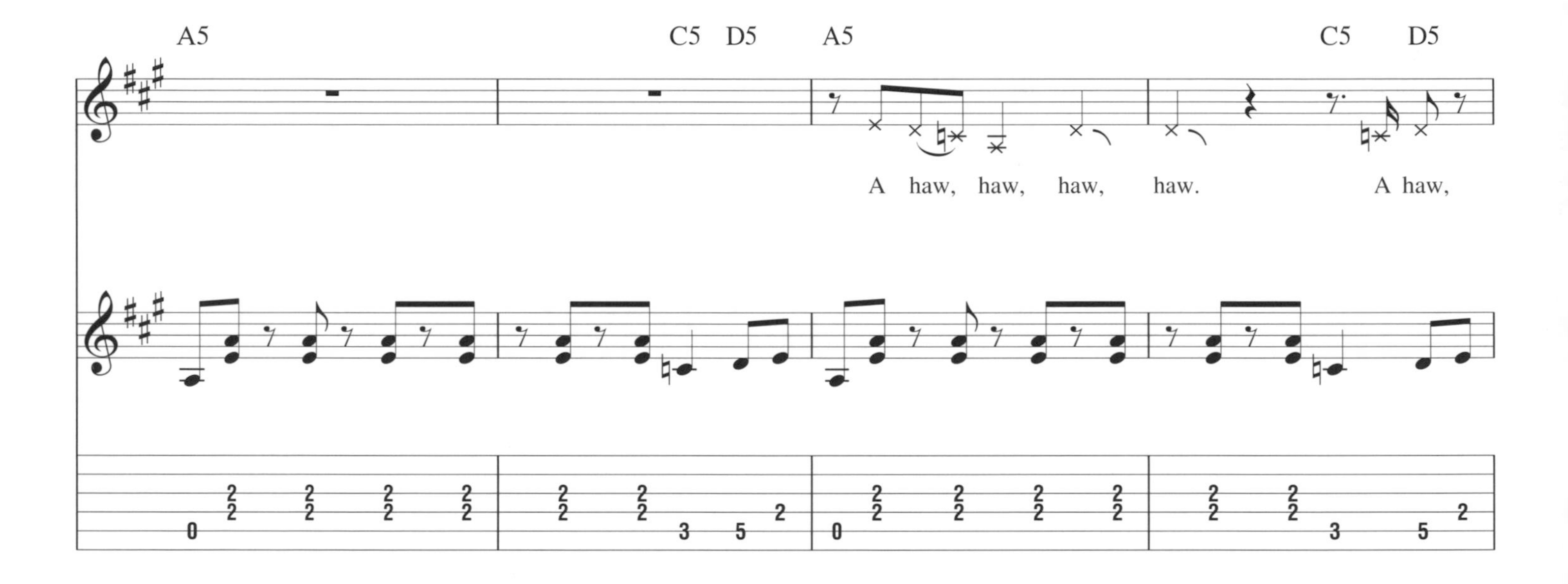
A5
C5 D5
A5
C5 D5
A haw, haw, haw, haw.
A haw,

Verse

A5
C5 D5
A5
C5 D5
a haw, haw, haw.
1. Well, I hear it's fine,
if you got the time

A5
C5 D5
A5
C5 D5
and the ten to get your - self in
0 2 2 2 2 2 2 2 2
2 2 2 2 3 5 2
0 2 2 2 2 2 2 2 2
2 2 2 2 3 5 2

A5
C5 D5
A5
C5 D5
a, hmm, hmm. And I hear it's tight most ev - er - y night,
0 2 2 2 2 2 2 2 2
2 2 2 2 3 5 2
0 2 2 2 2 2 2 2 2
2 2 2 2 3 5 2

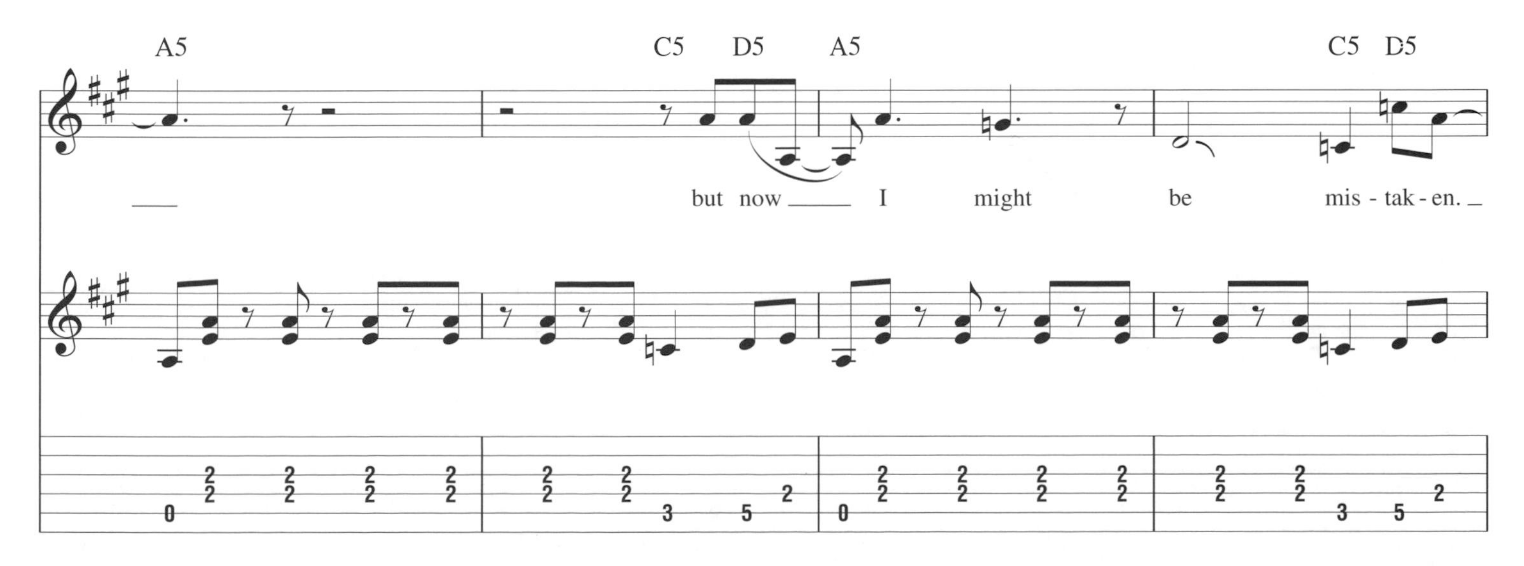
A5
C5 D5
A5
C5 D5
but now I might be mis - tak - en.
0 2 2 2 2 2 2 2 2
2 2 2 2 3 5 2
0 2 2 2 2 2 2 2 2
2 2 2 2 3 5 2

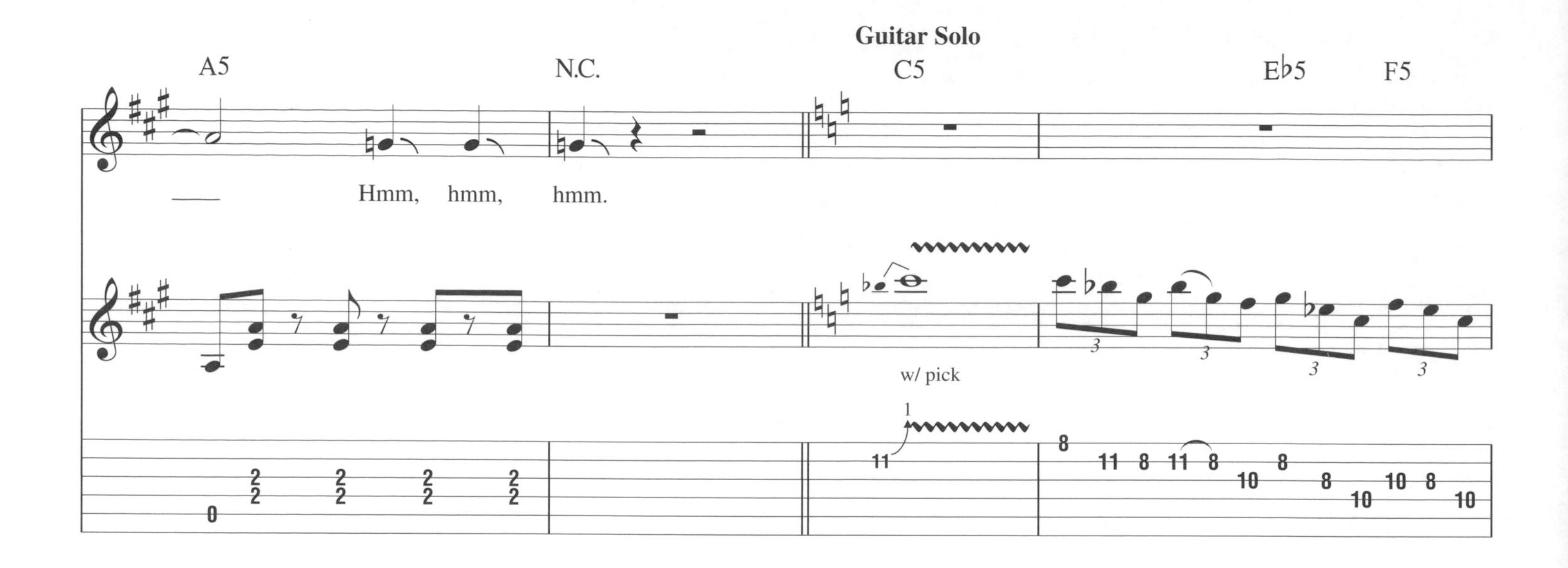
Guitar Solo
A5
N.C.
C5
E♭5
F5
Hmm, hmm, hmm.
w/ pick

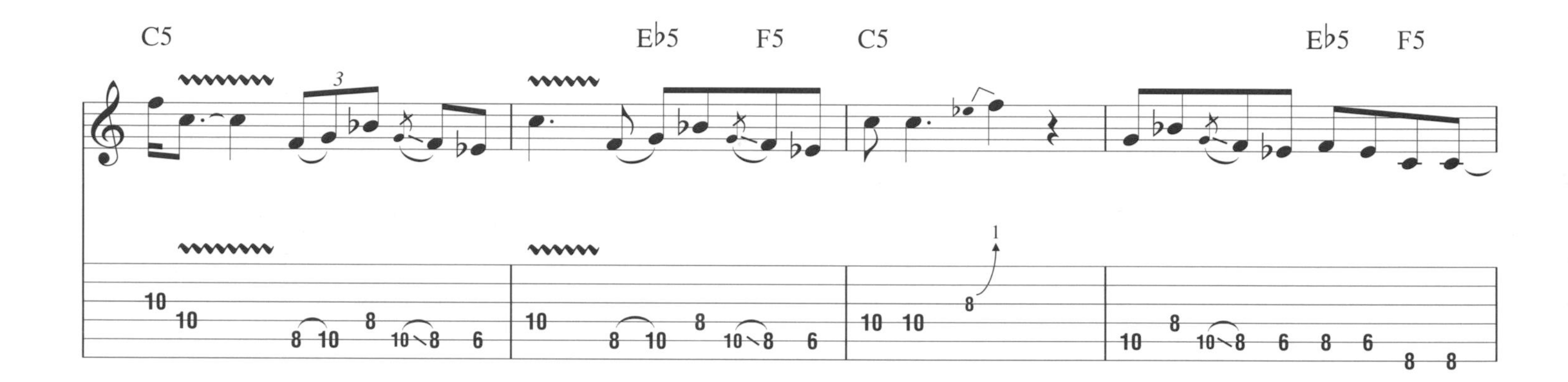
C5
E♭5
F5
C5
E♭5
F5

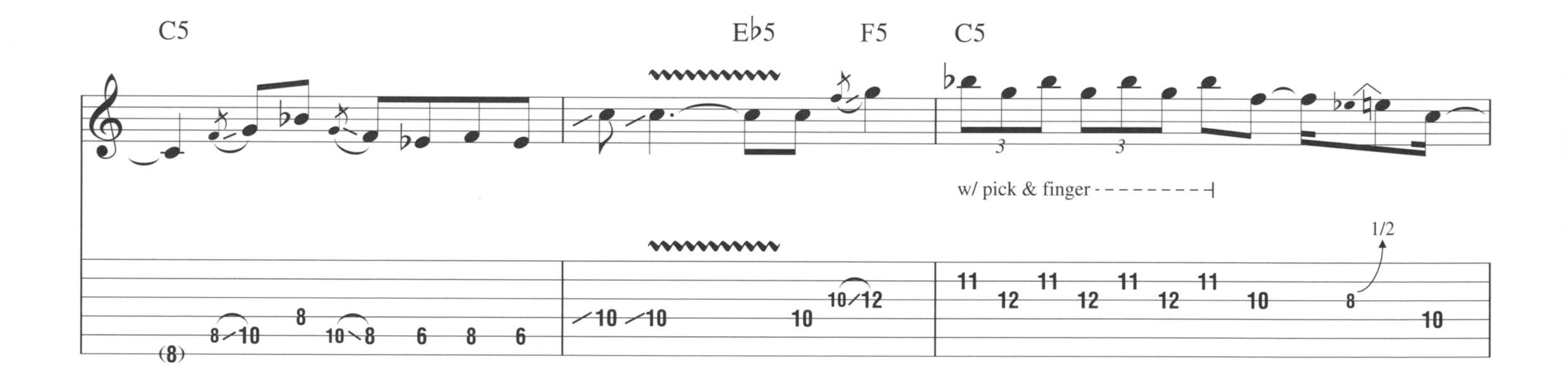
C5
E♭5
F5
C5
w/ pick & finger

E♭5
F5
C5
E♭5
F5

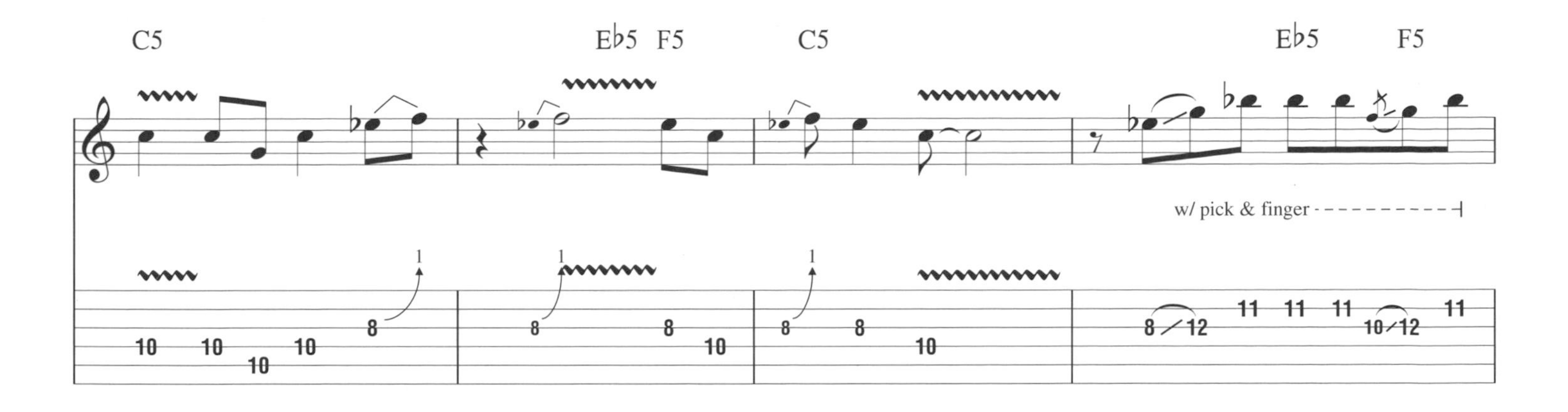
C5
E♭5 F5
C5
E♭5 F5
w/ pick & finger

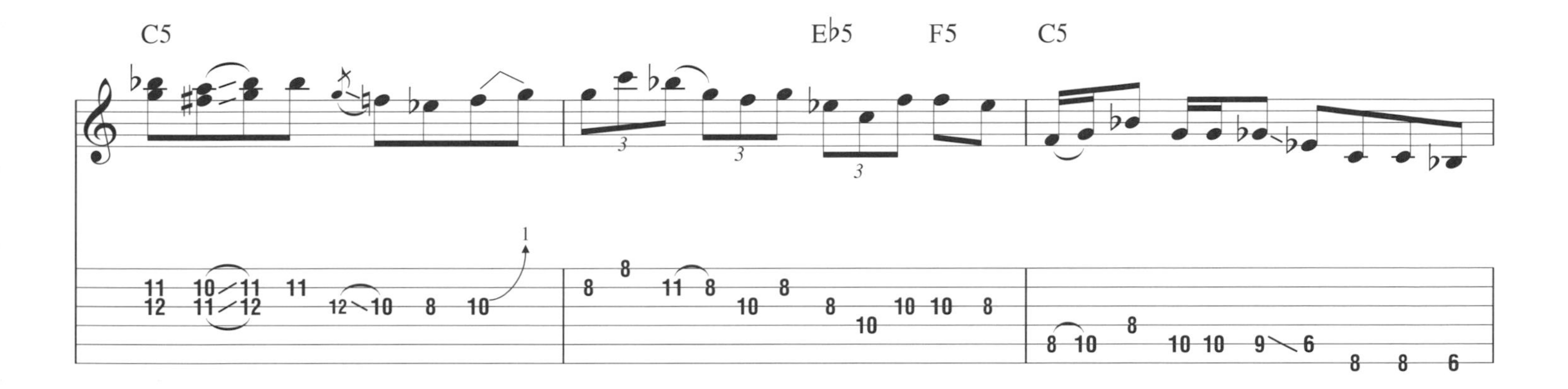
C5
E♭5 F5
C5

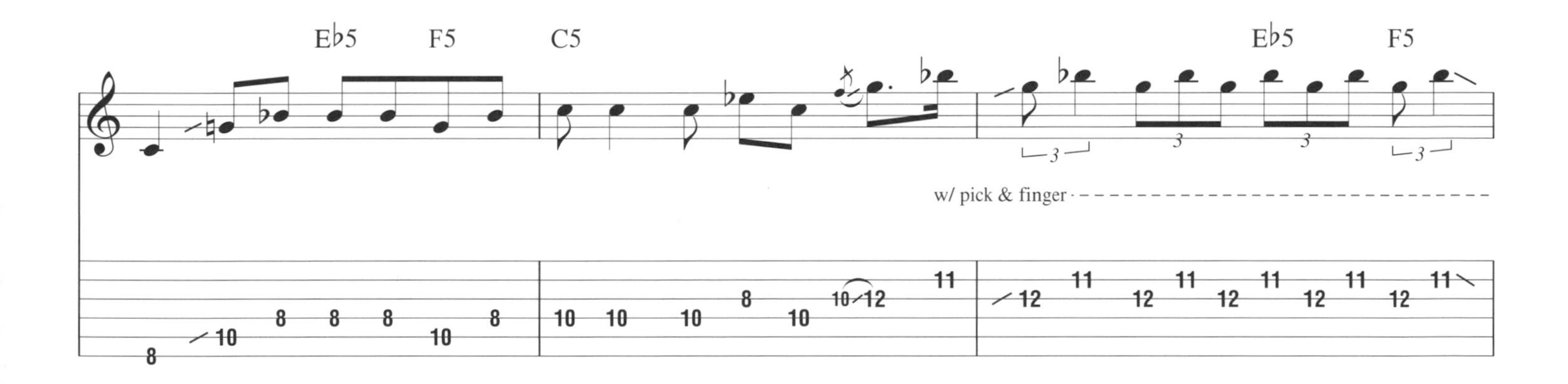
E♭5 F5
C5
E♭5 F5
w/ pick & finger

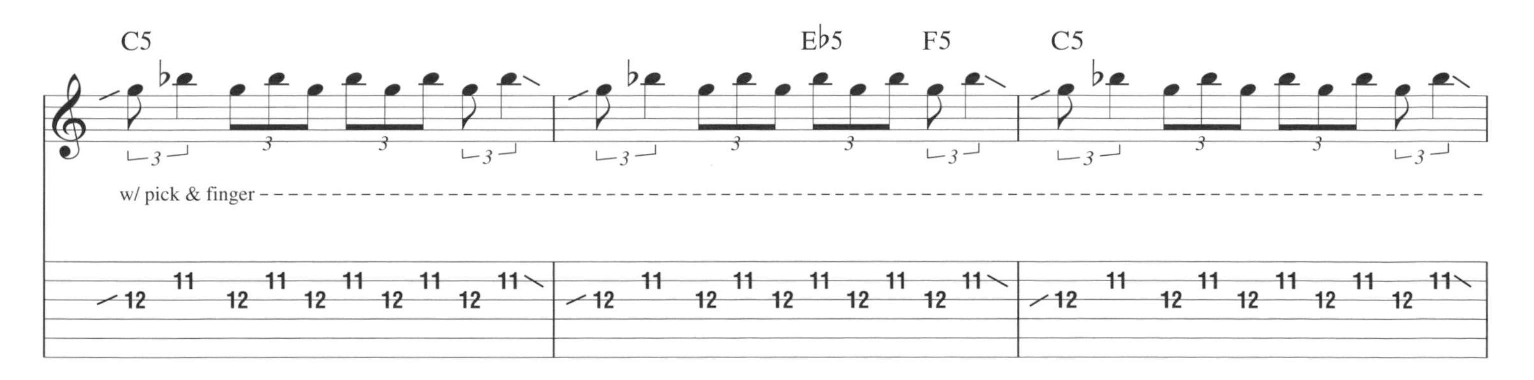
C5
E♭5 F5
C5
w/ pick & finger

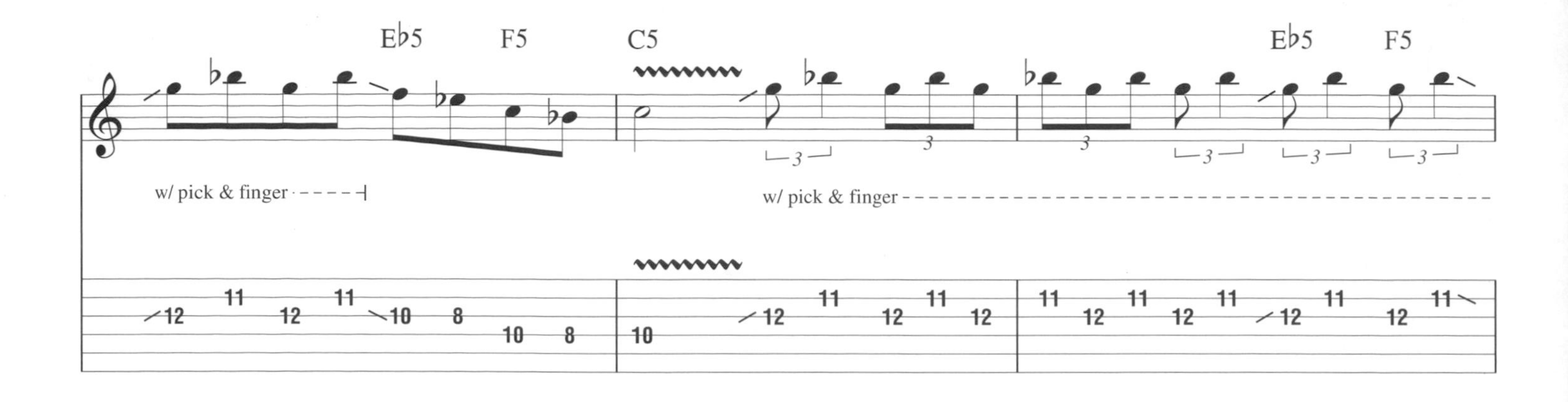
E♭5
F5
C5
E♭5
F5
w/ pick & finger
w/ pick & finger

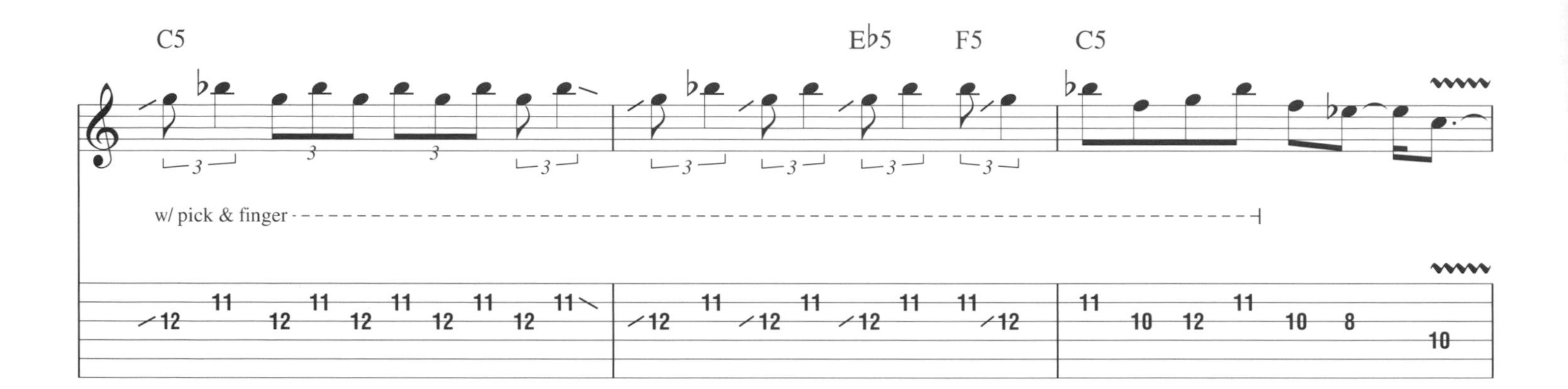
C5
E♭5
F5
C5
w/ pick & finger

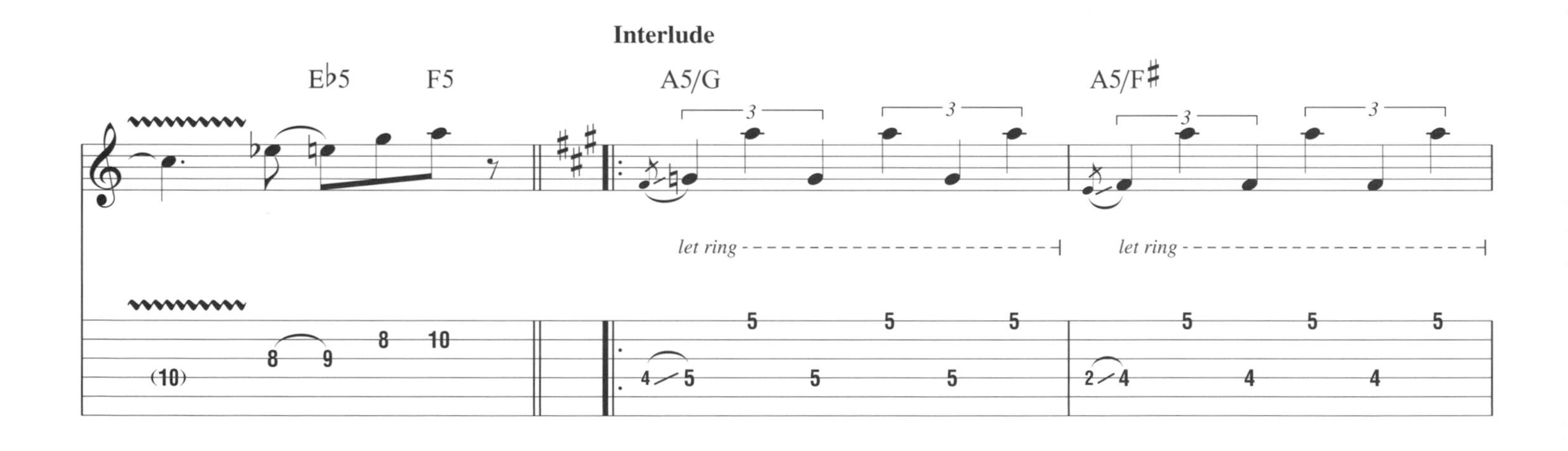
Interlude
E♭5
F5
A5/G
A5/F♯
let ring
let ring

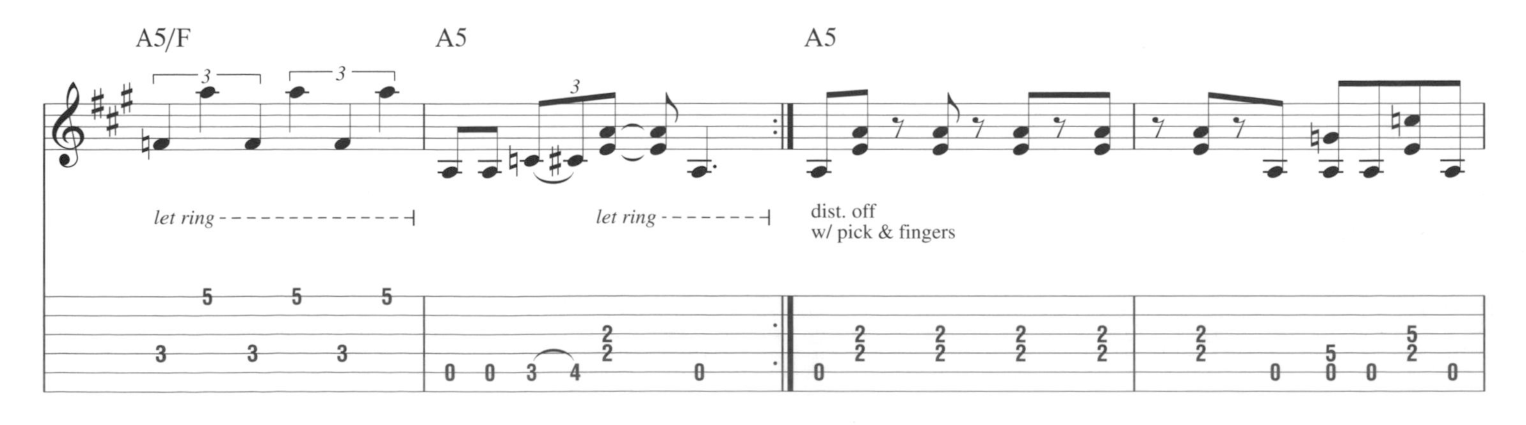
A5/F
A5
A5
let ring
let ring
dist. off
w/ pick & fingers

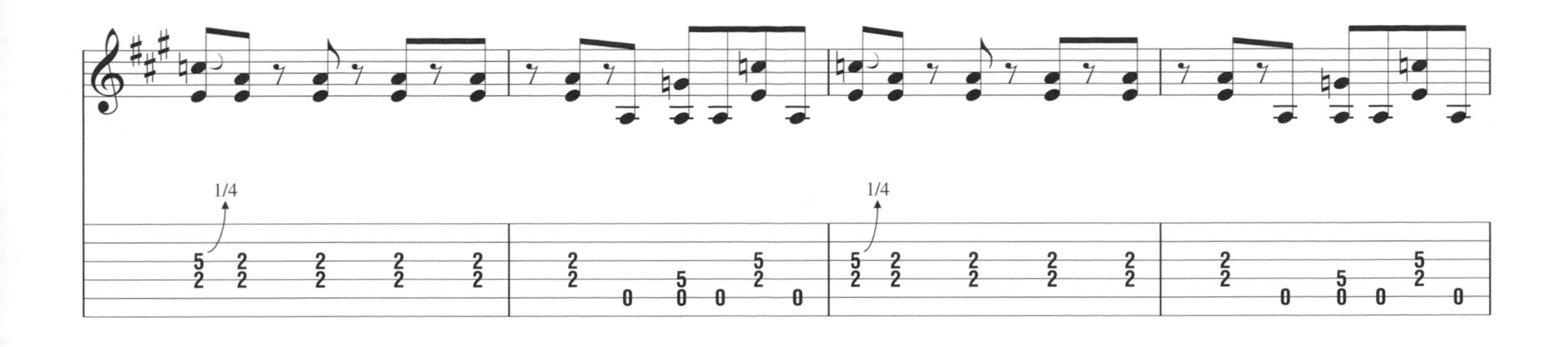

Outro-Guitar Solo

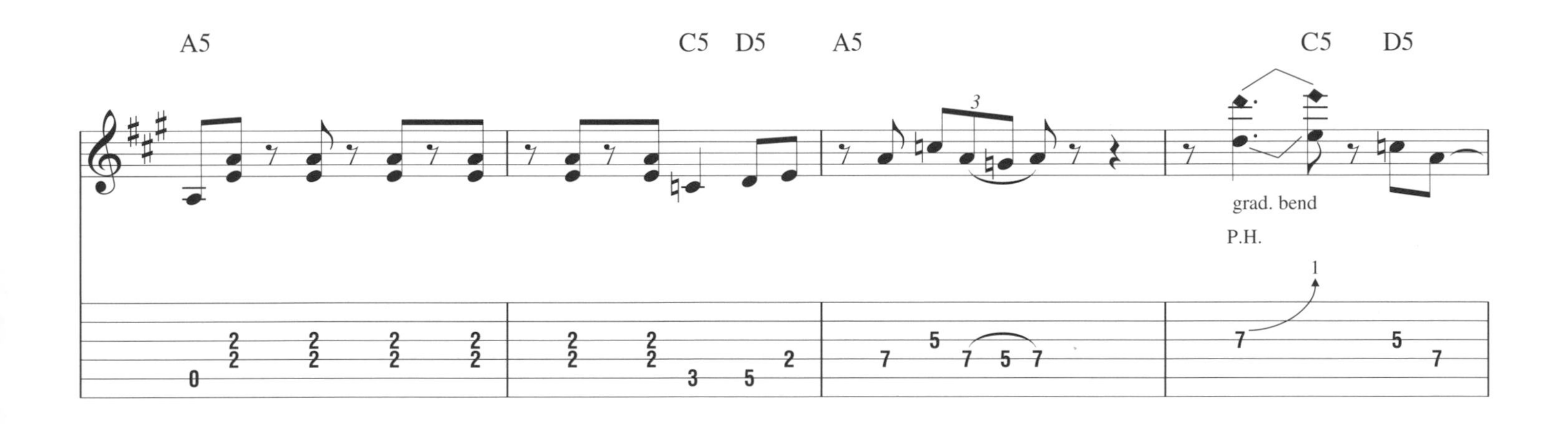

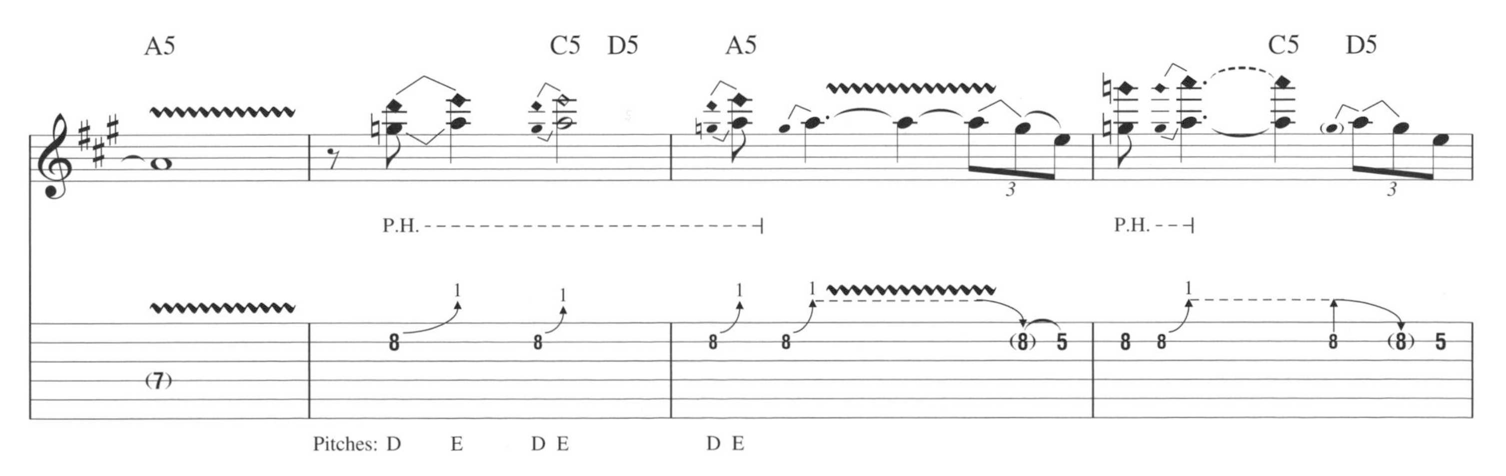

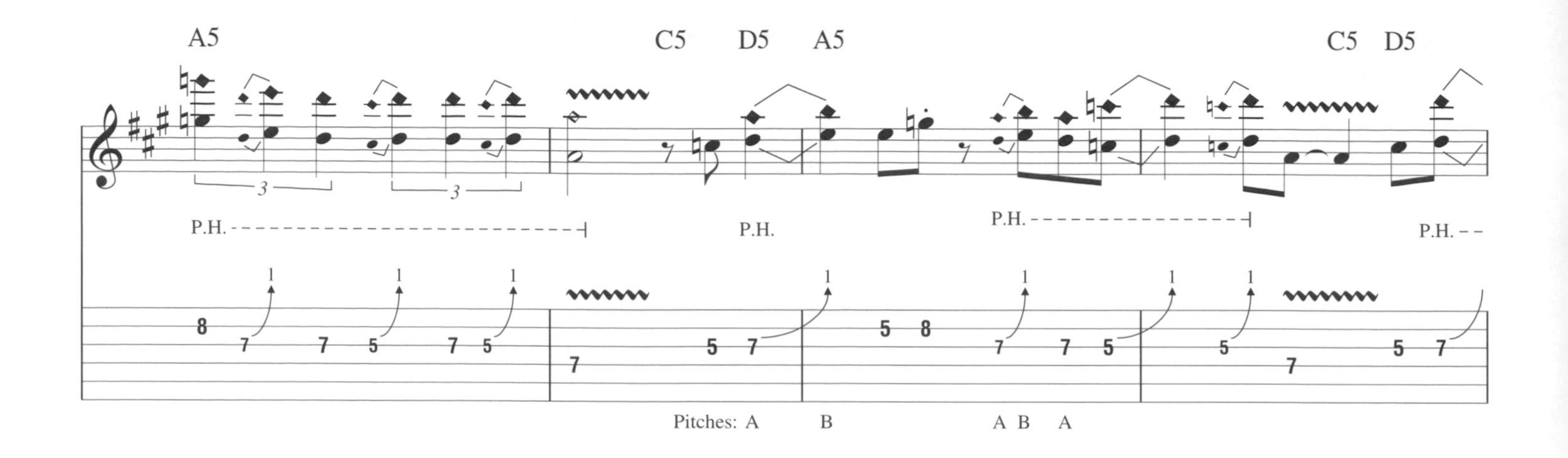
A5
C5
D5
A5
C5
D5
P.H.
P.H.
P.H.
P.H.
Pitches: A
B
A B
A

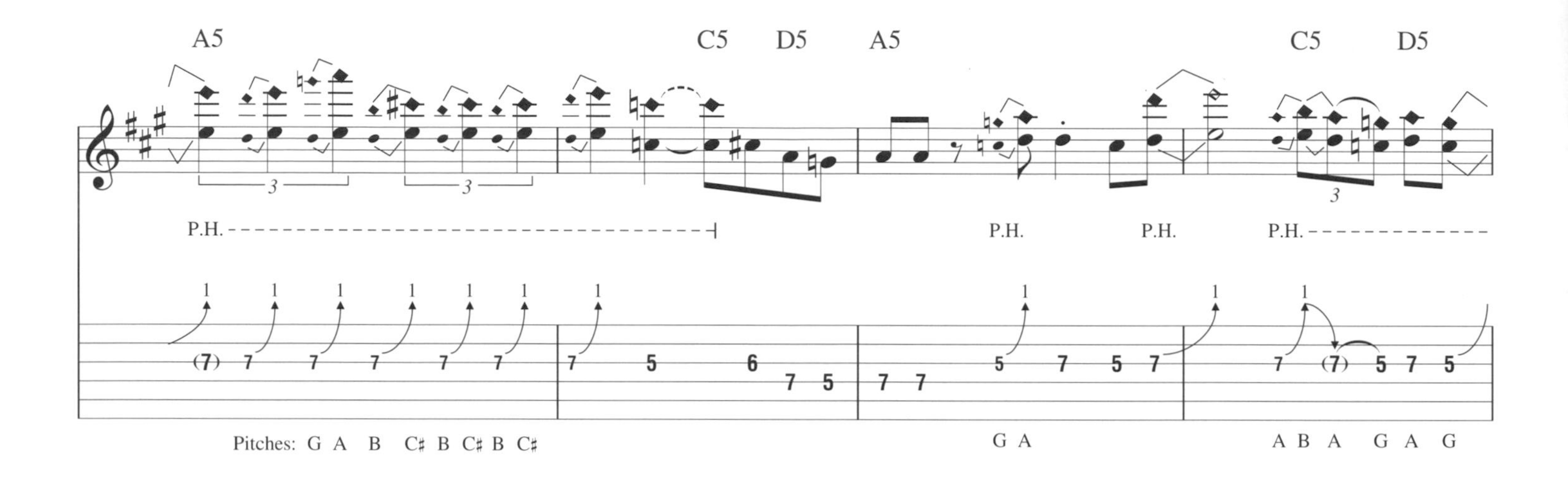
A5
C5
D5
A5
C5
D5
P.H.
P.H.
P.H.
P.H.
Pitches: G A B C♯ B C♯ B C♯
G A
A B A G A G

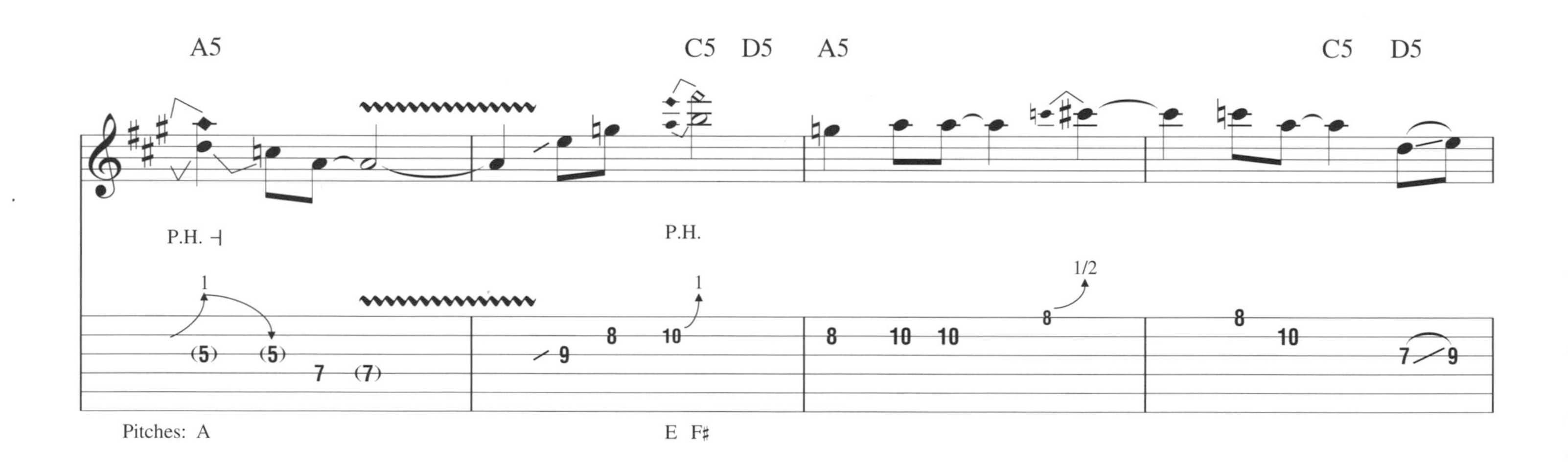
A5
C5
D5
A5
C5
D5
P.H.
P.H.
Pitches: A
E F♯

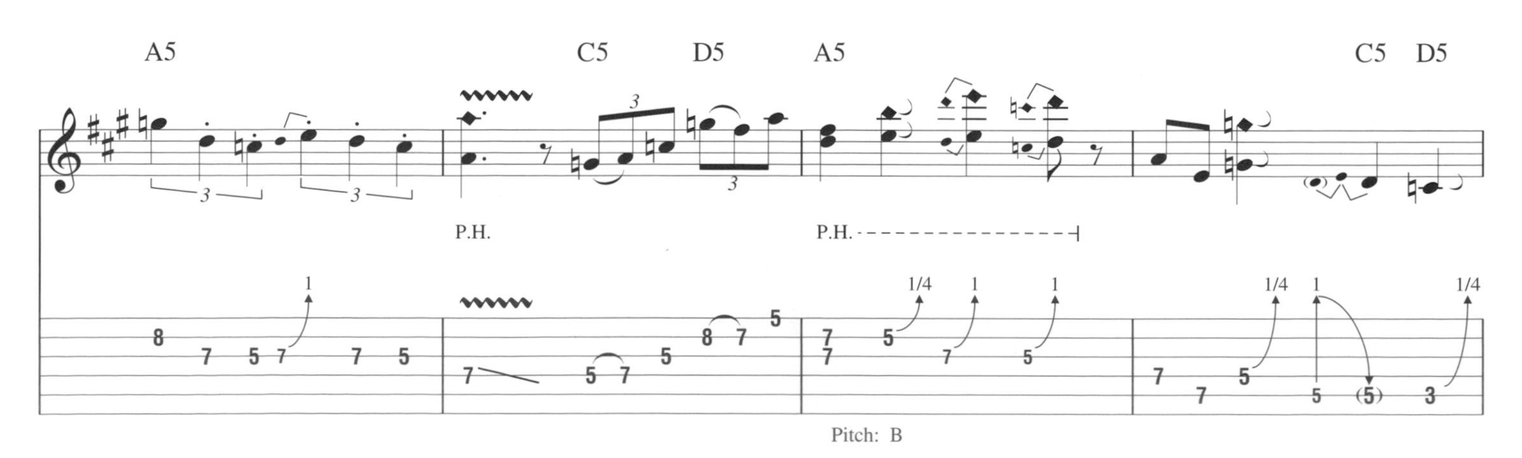
A5
C5
D5
A5
C5
D5
P.H.
P.H.
Pitch: B

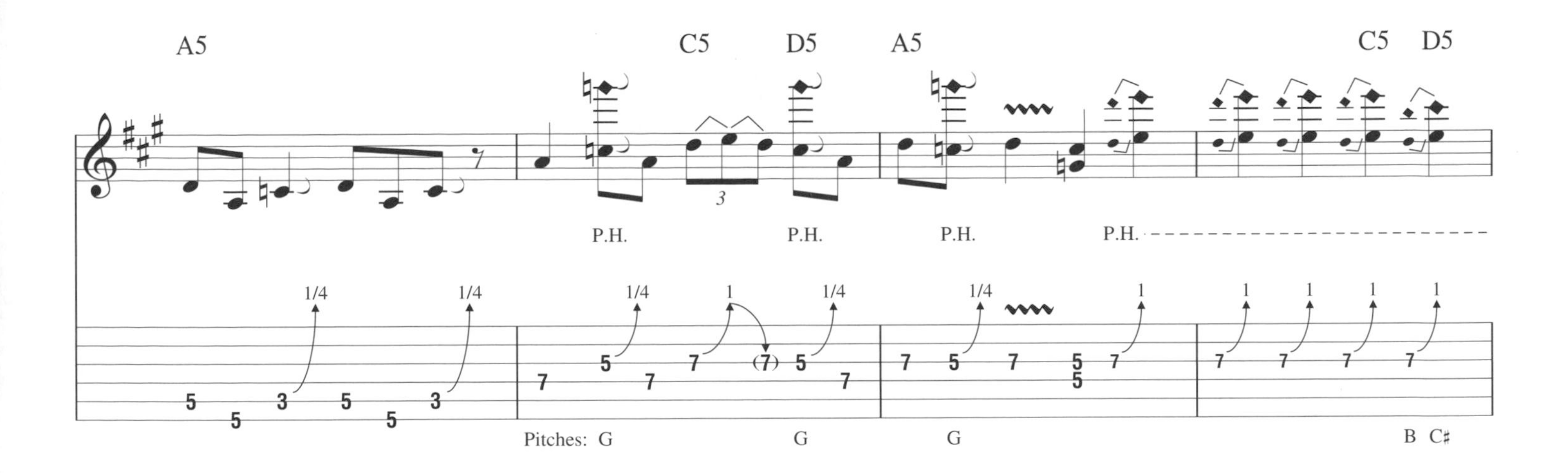

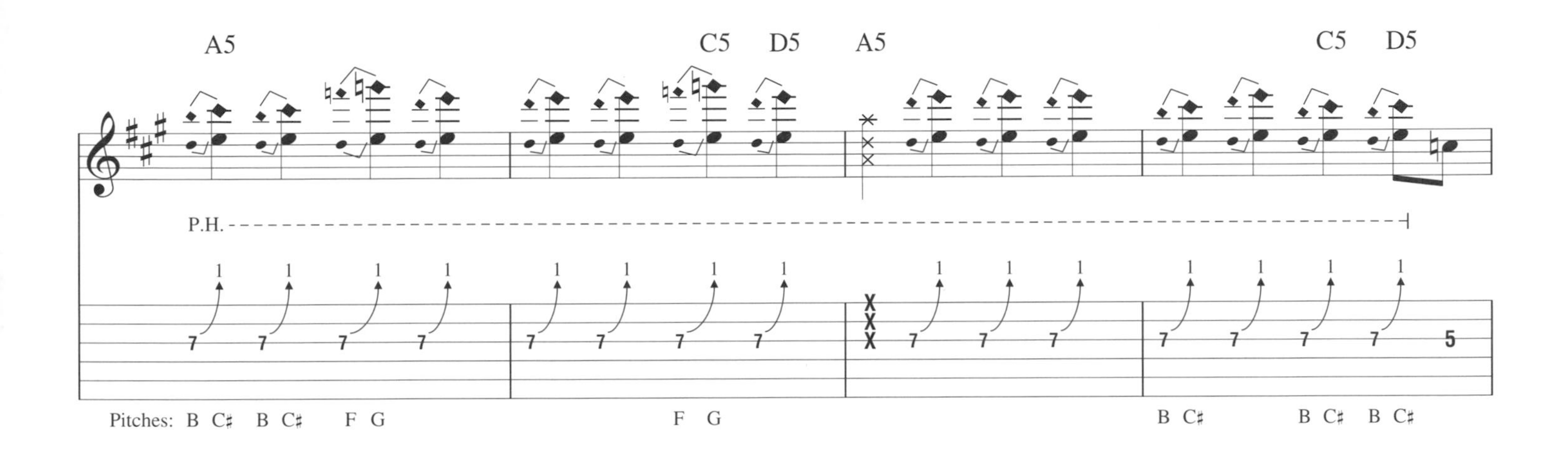

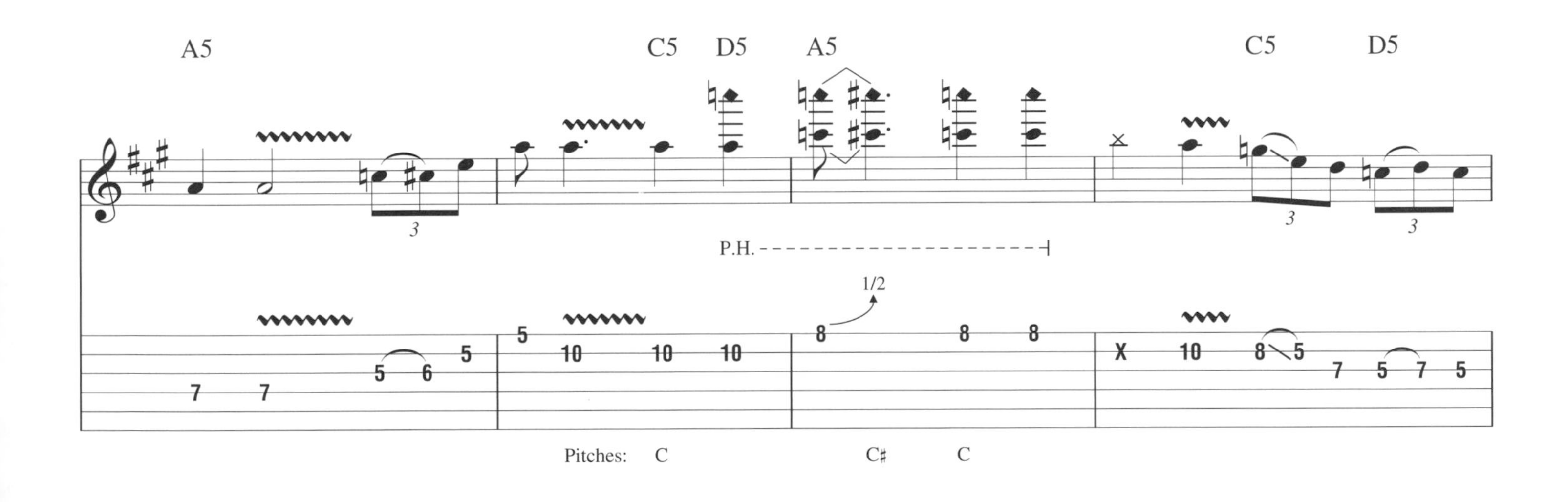

Repeat and fade

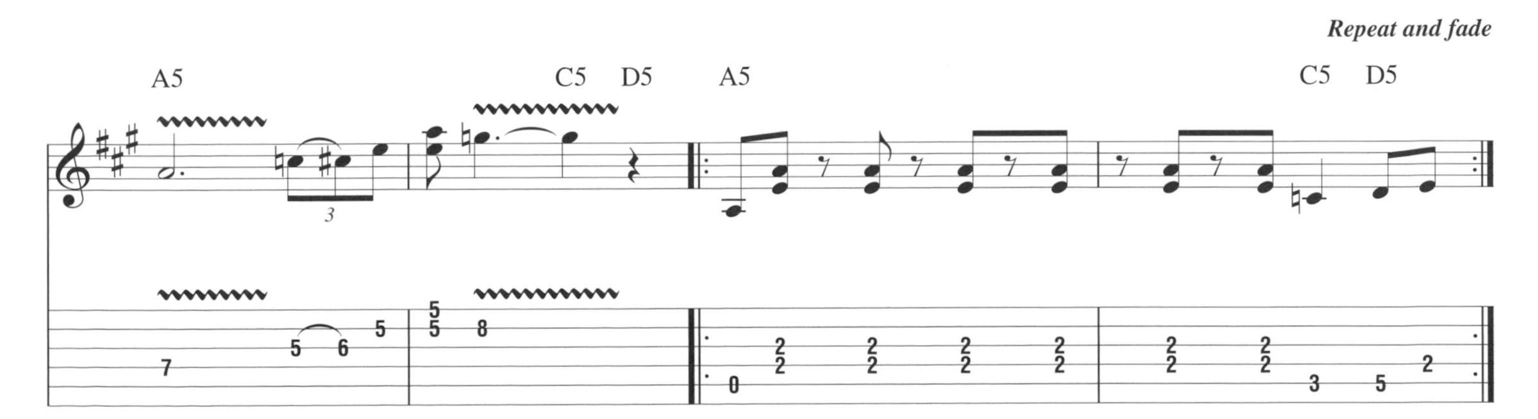

Legs

Words and Music by Billy F Gibbons, Dusty Hill and Frank Lee Beard

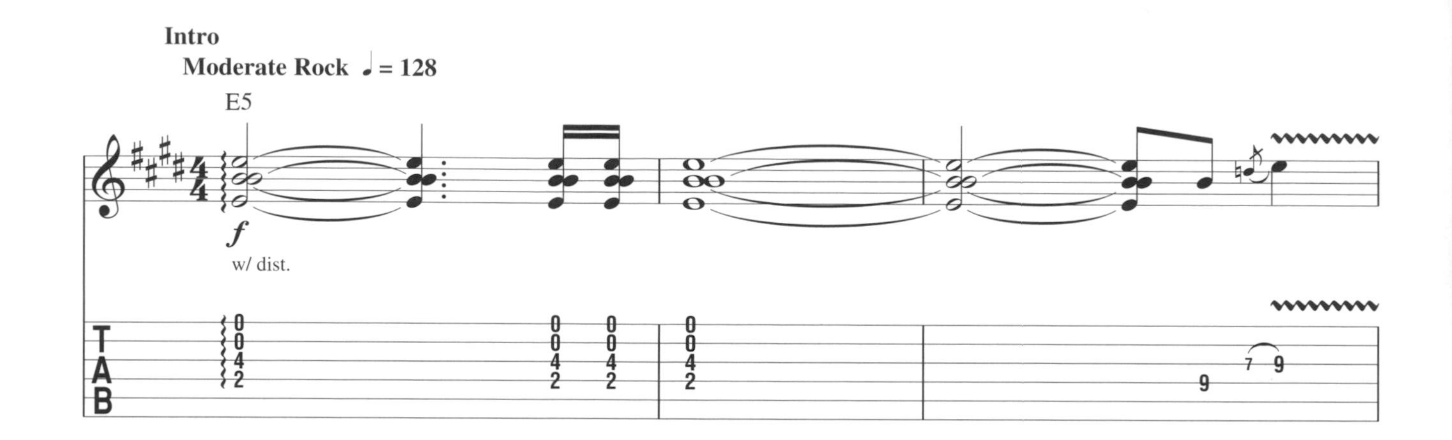

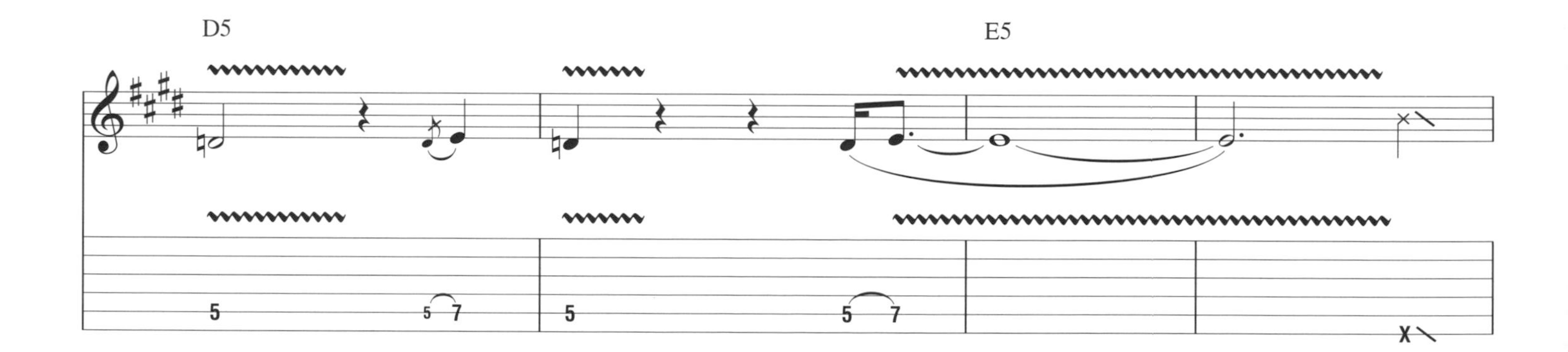

1. She got
0 5 4
2

E5
legs,
she knows how to use them.
P.H.

C♯5
She nev - er begs,
she knows how to
semi-harm.

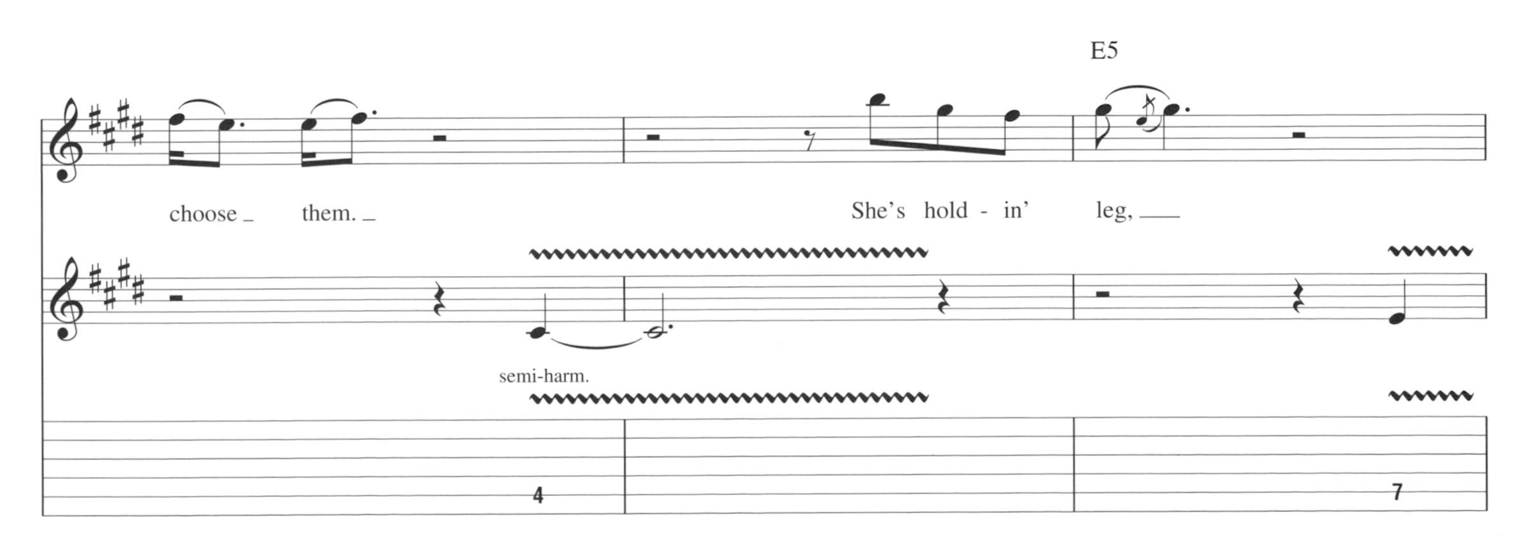
E5
choose them.
She's hold - in' leg,
semi-harm.

wonder how to feel them.
Would you get behind them
if you could only find them?
P.M.
semi-harm.
C#5
A5
She's my baby,
she's my baby,
B5
yeah, and it's al-

Interlude
E
right.
Oh,

yeah.
2. She's got

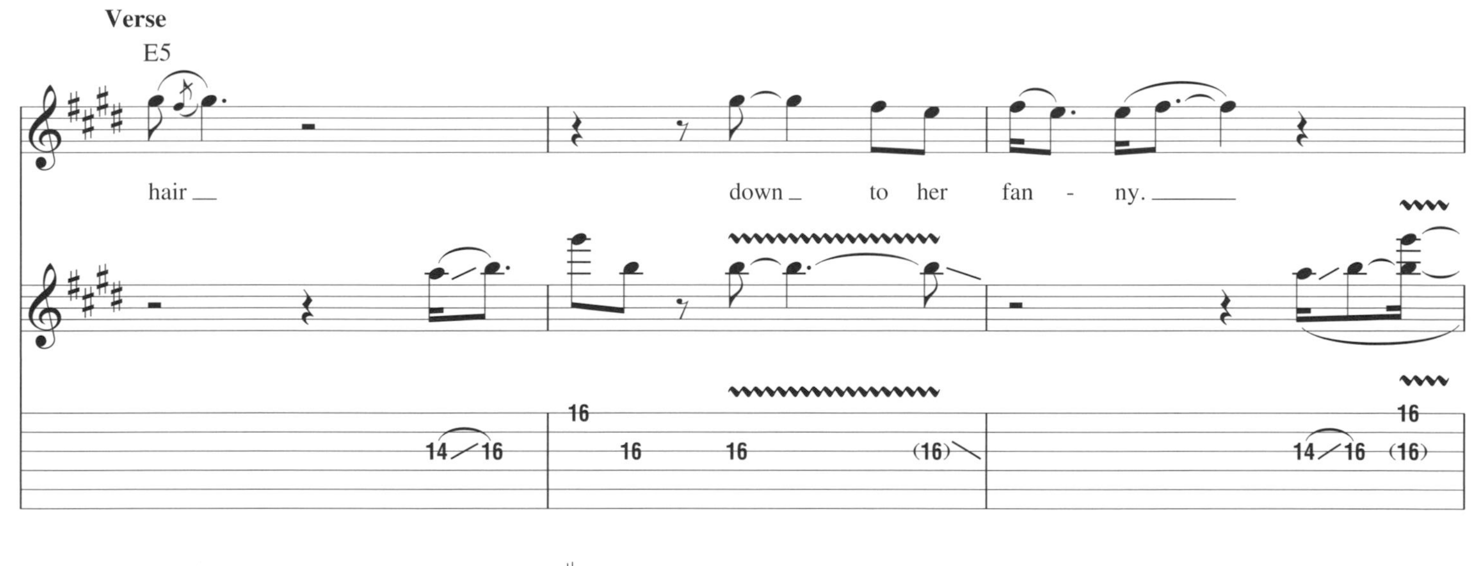
Verse
E5
hair
down to her
fan - ny.

C♯5
She kind - a
jet set,
try and un - do her

*Tap from nowhere with pick hand index finger.

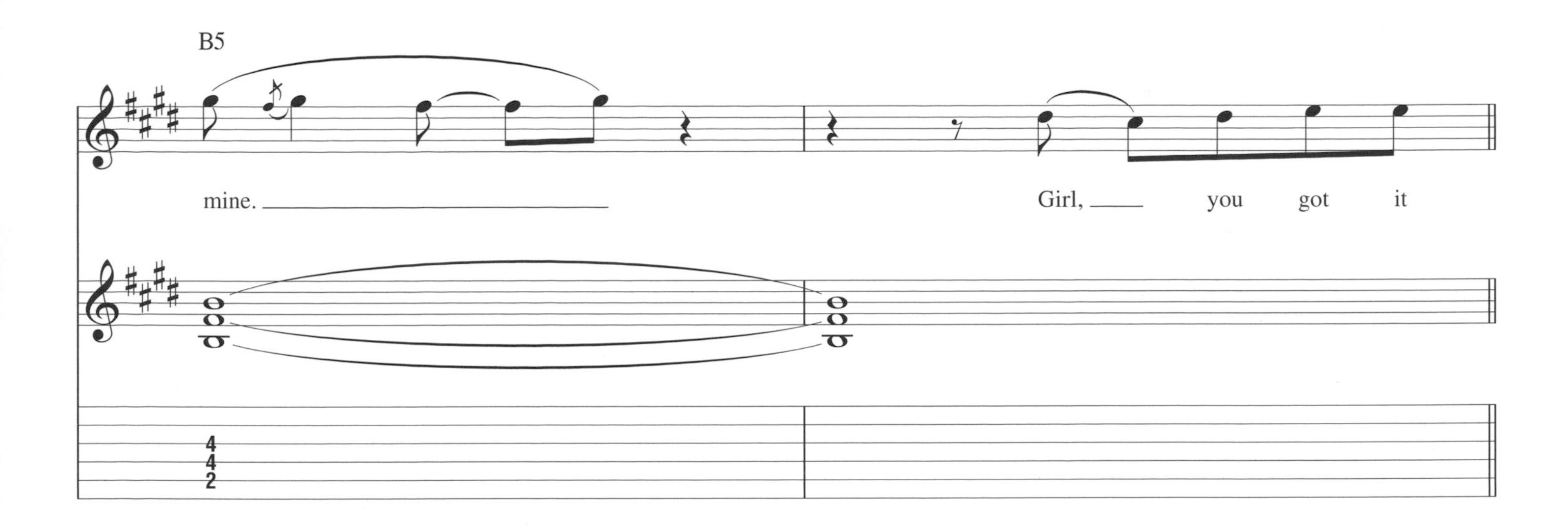

Interlude

E

right.

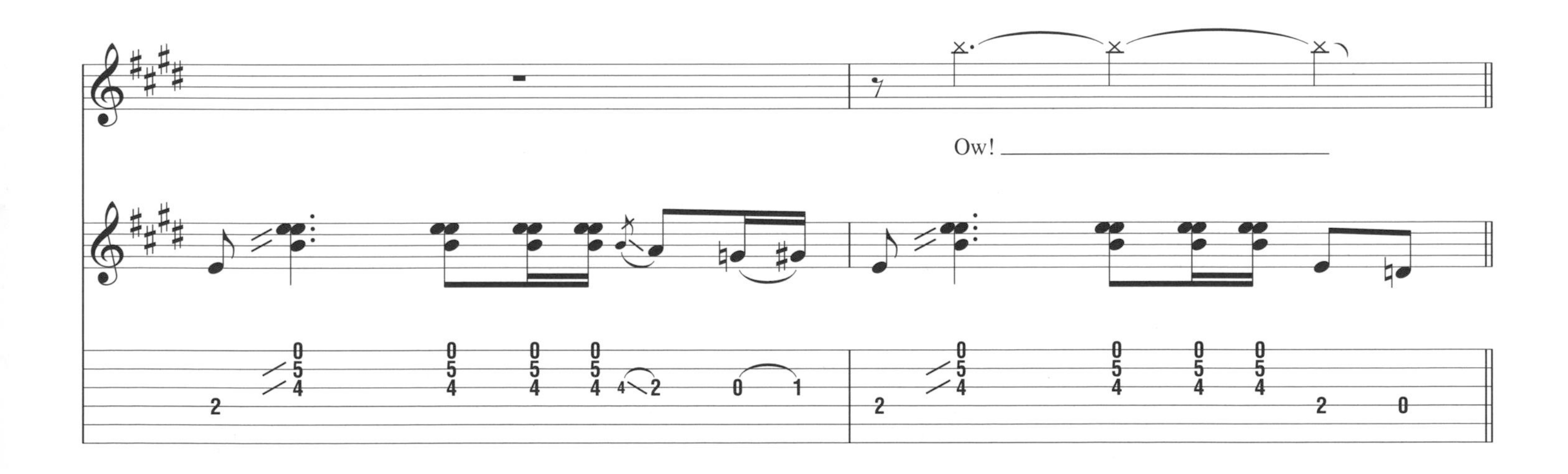

Guitar Solo

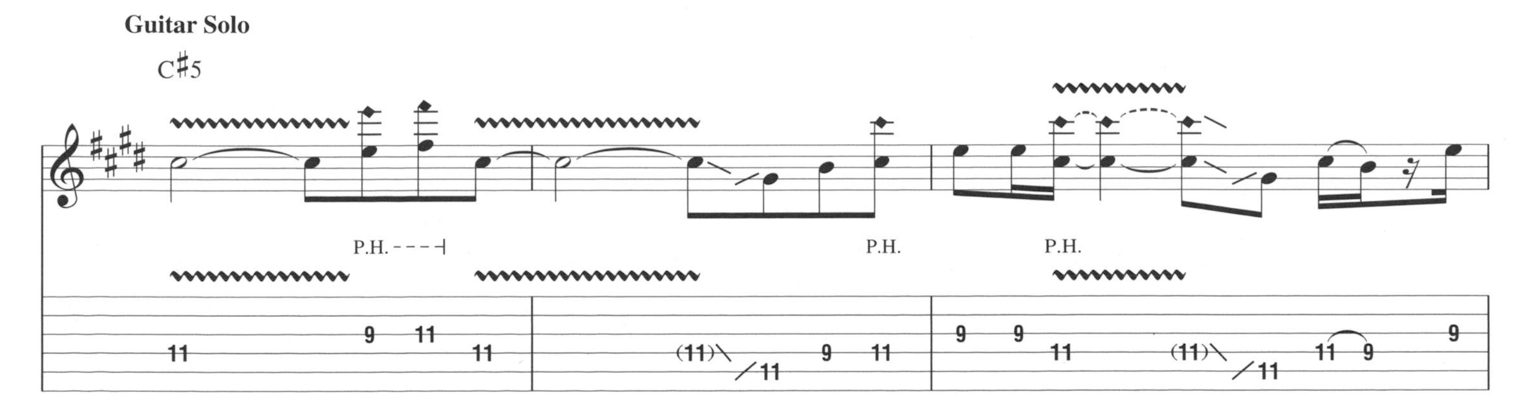

F♯5
P.H.
rake
P.H.
P.H.

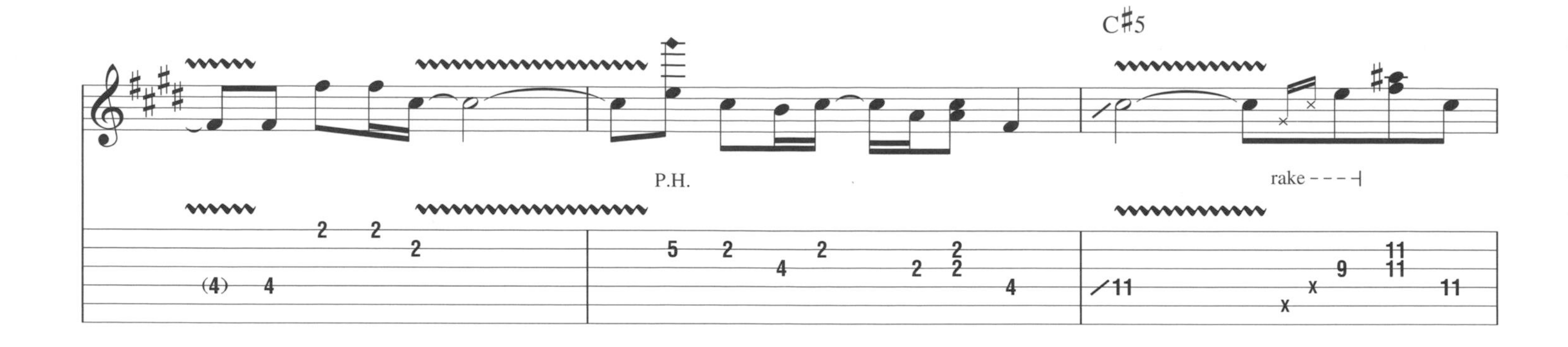
C♯5
P.H.
rake

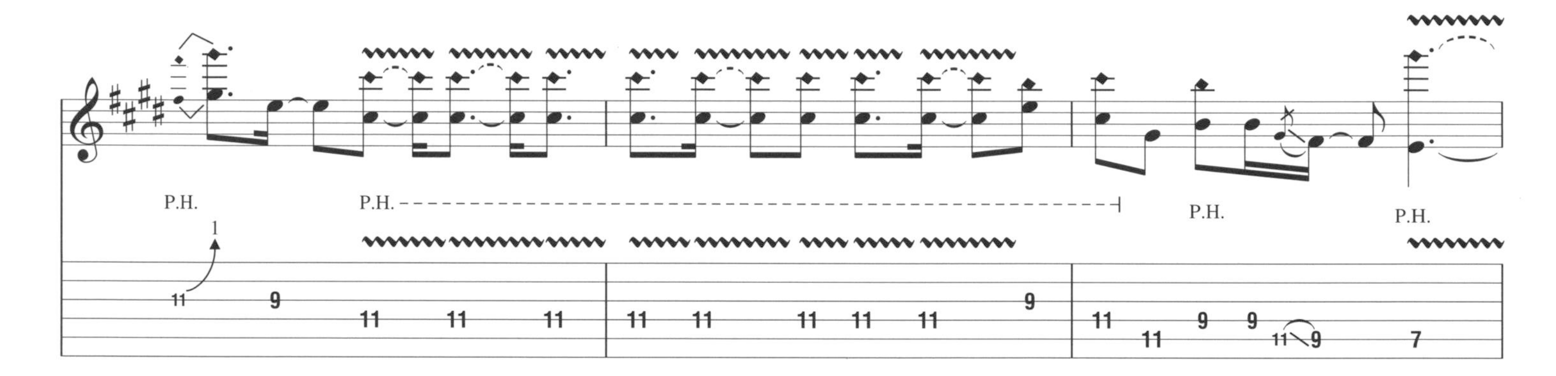
P.H.
P.H.
P.H.
P.H.

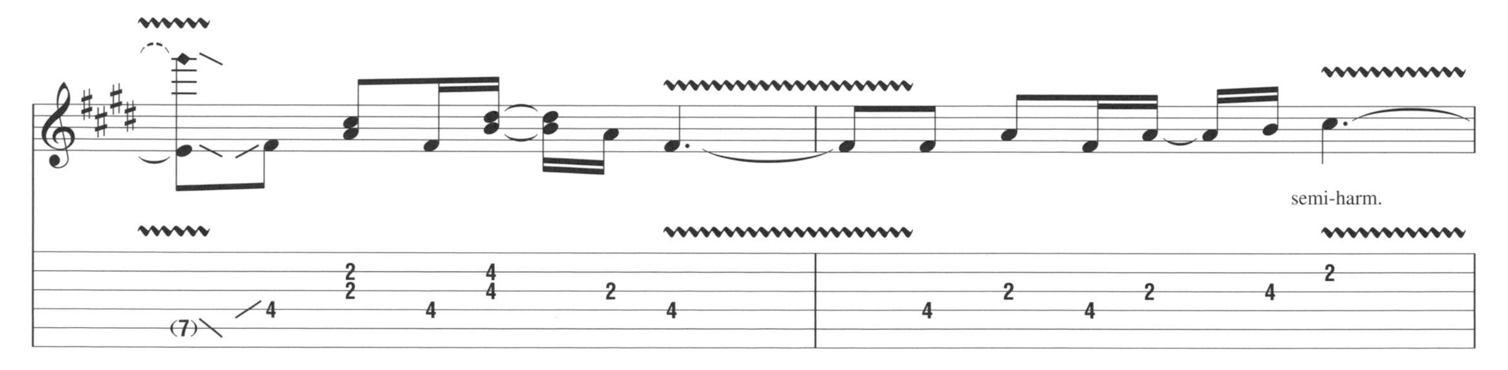
F♯5
semi-harm.

B
Bsus4
B
Bsus4
B
let ring
let ring

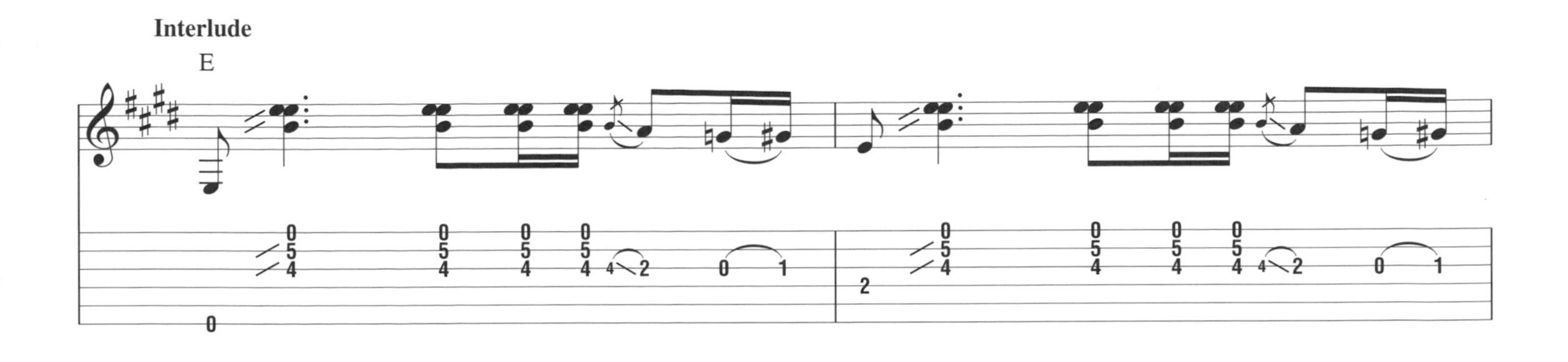
Interlude
E

She got

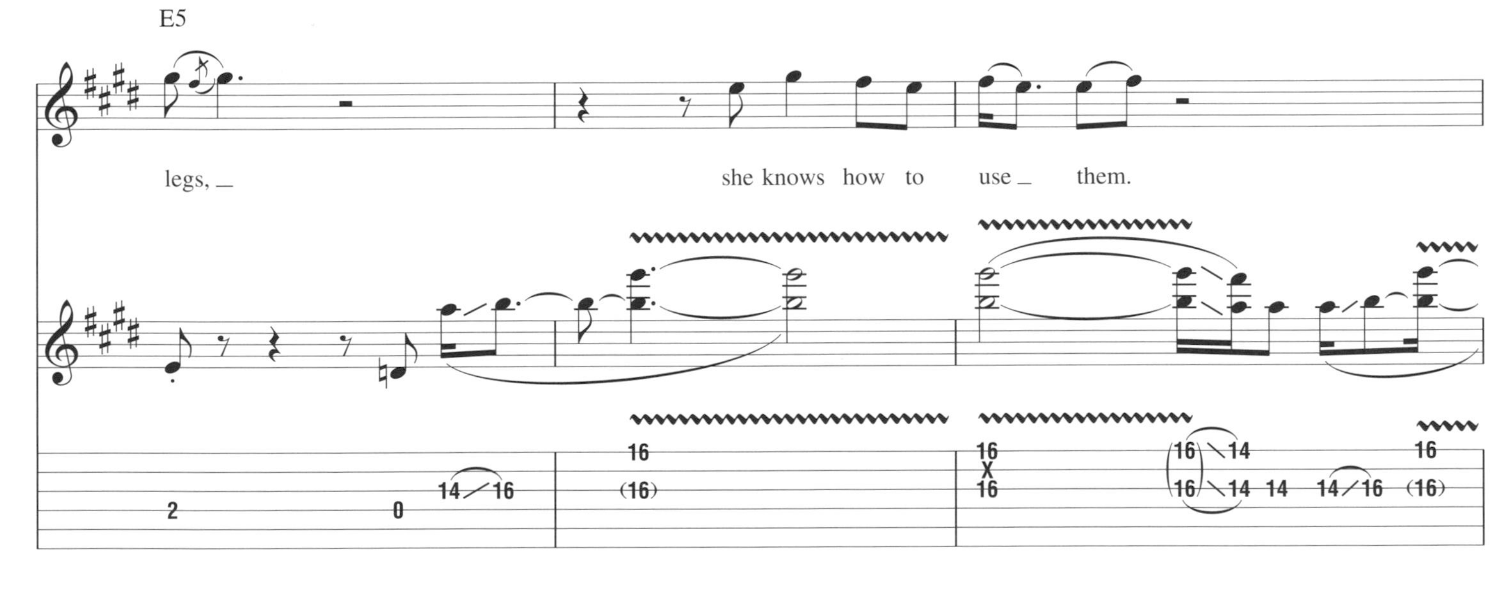
Verse
E5
legs, she knows how to use them.

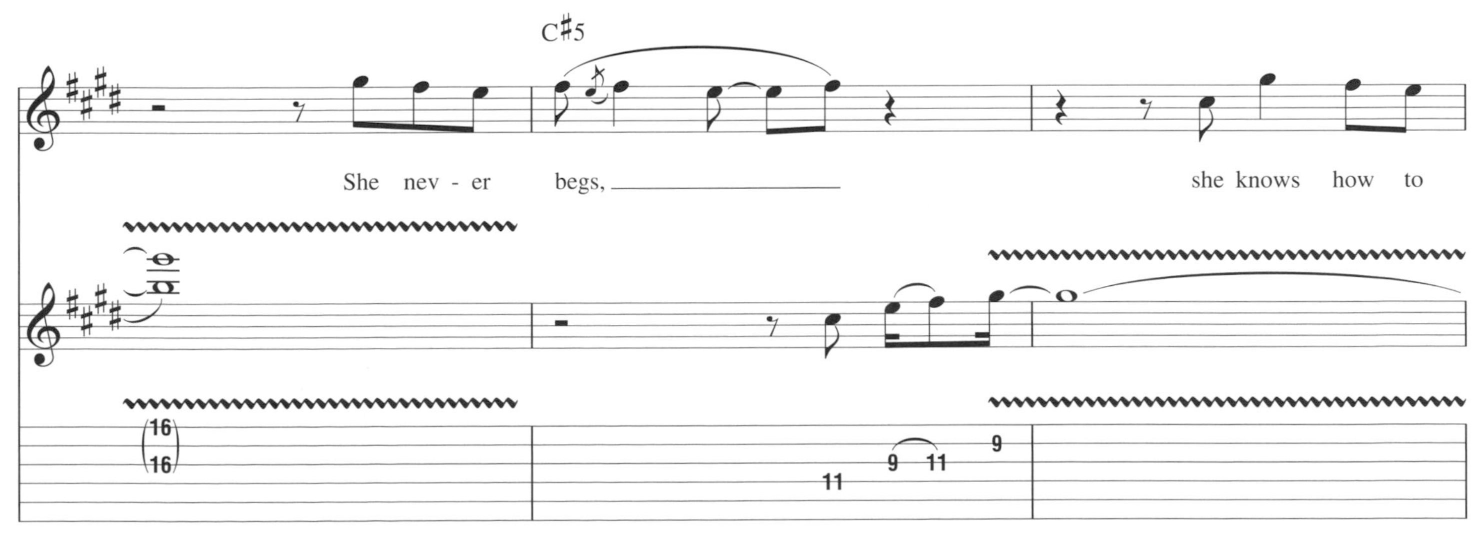
C♯5
She nev - er begs, she knows how to

E5
choose _ them. _
She got a dime _
all of the time.
Stays out at
C#5
night,
mov - in' through time.
P.H. P.H.
A5
Whoa, I want _ her, _
shit, I got to

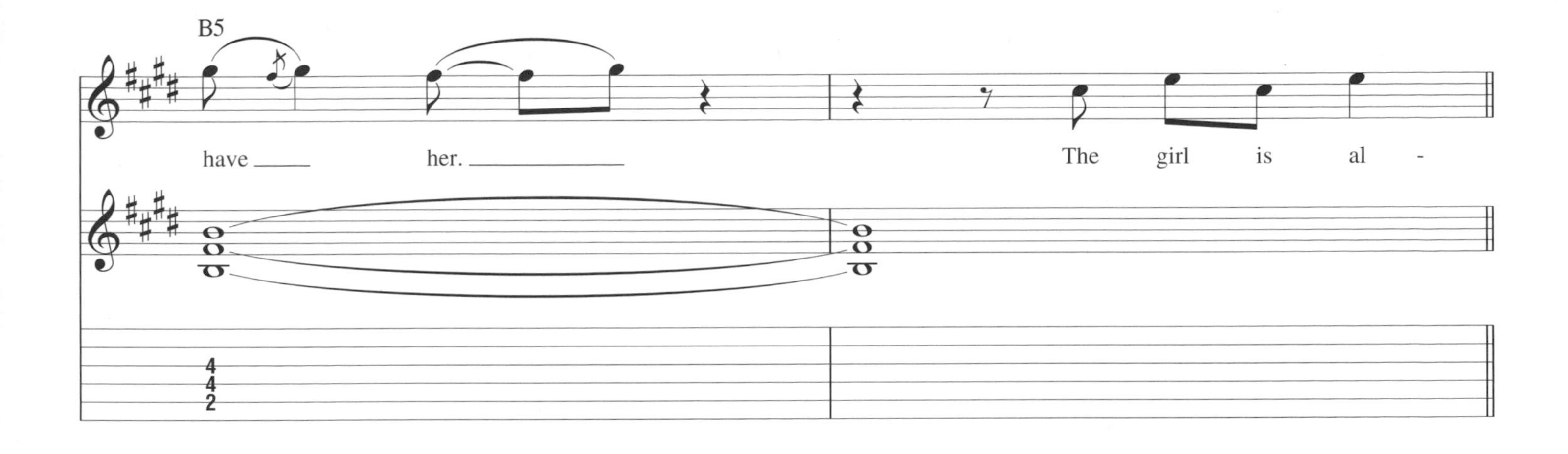
B5
have her.
The girl is al -

Interlude
E
right,
she's al -

right.
Whoa.

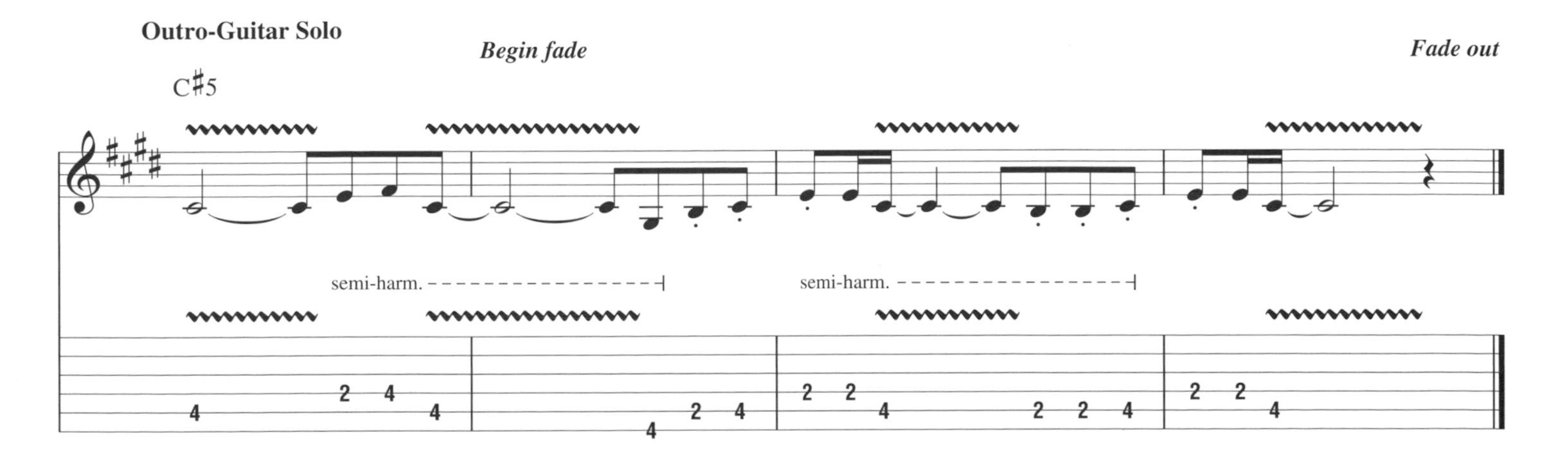
Outro-Guitar Solo
Begin fade
Fade out
C♯5
semi-harm.
semi-harm.

Sharp Dressed Man

Words and Music by Billy F Gibbons, Dusty Hill and Frank Lee Beard

C5
B♭5
go - in' to.
Silk suit,
black tie,
let ring
To Coda 2
Chorus
F5
G5
F5 G5
I don't need a rea - son why.
They come run - nin' just as
To Coda 1
B♭5/F C5/G
N.C.
E♭5 B♭5
fast as they can,
'cause ev - 'ry girl's cra - zy 'bout a sharp dressed man.
Interlude
Cm7
P.M.
let ring

D.S. al Coda 1

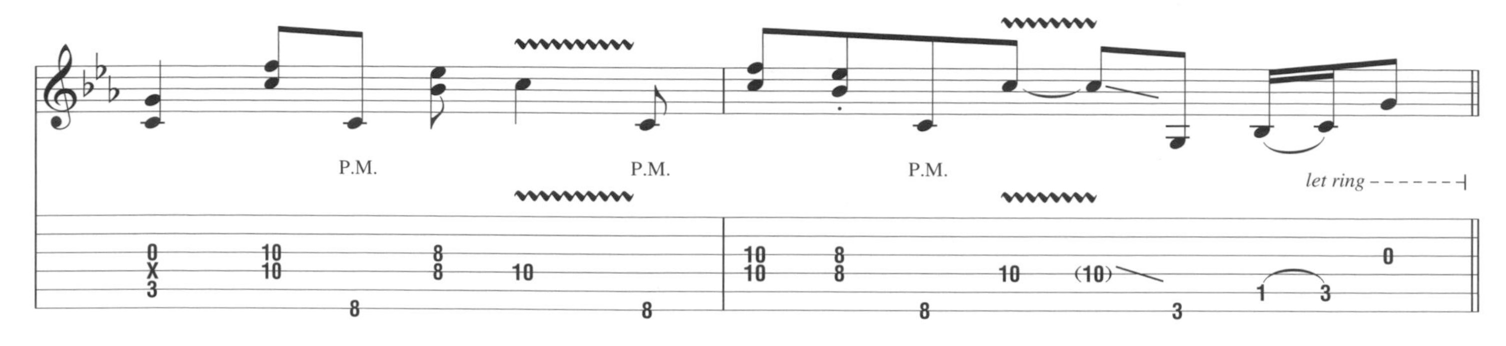

Coda 1

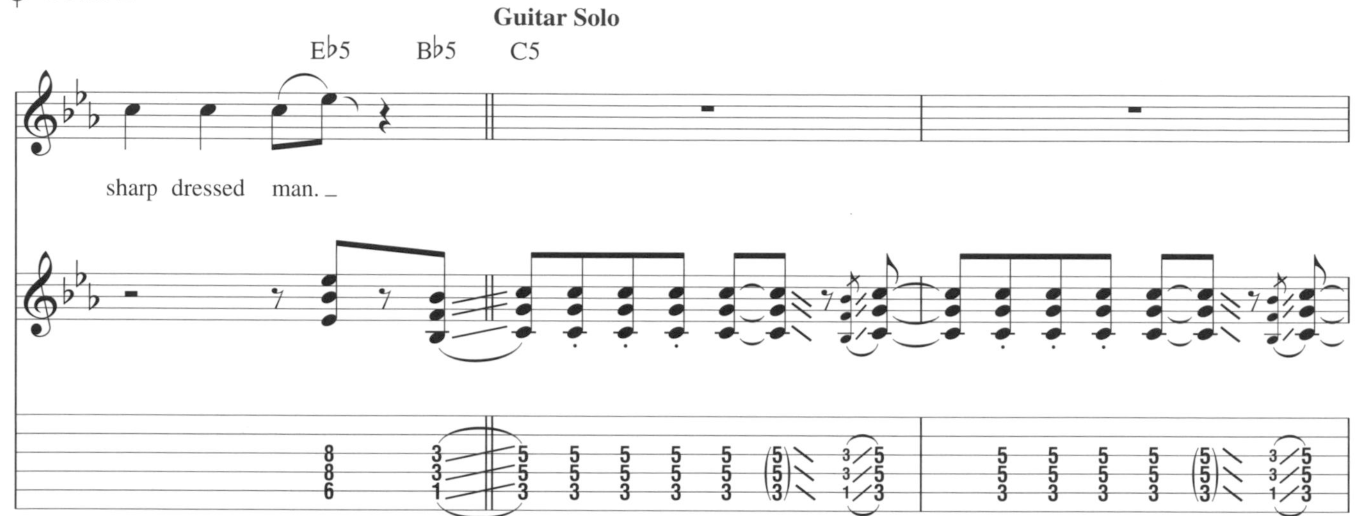

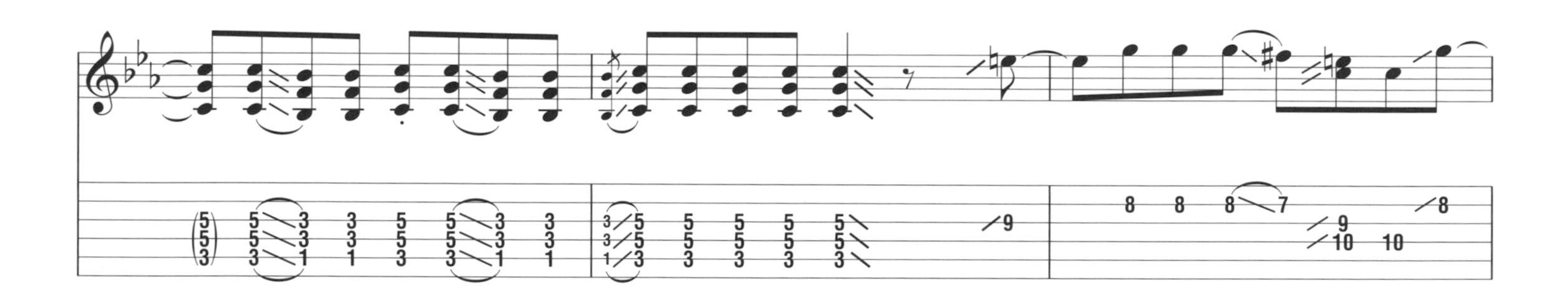

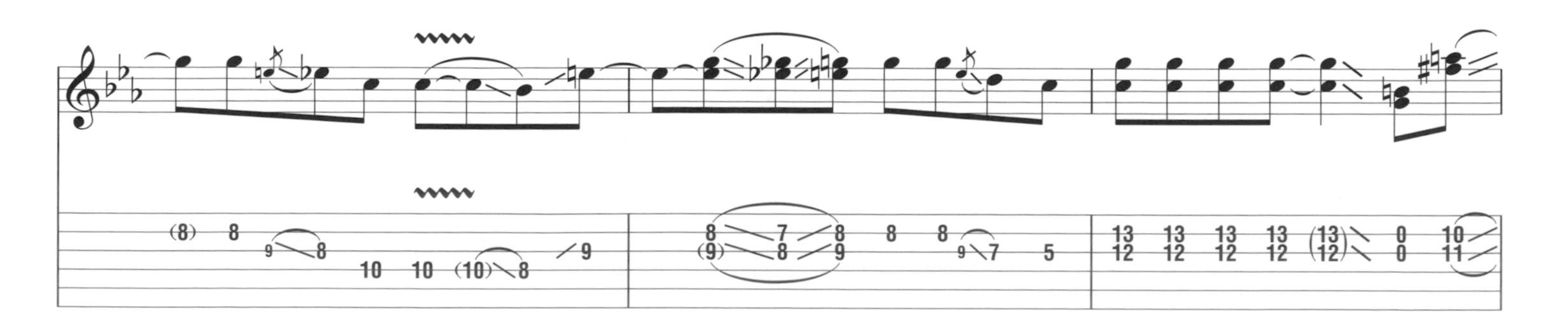

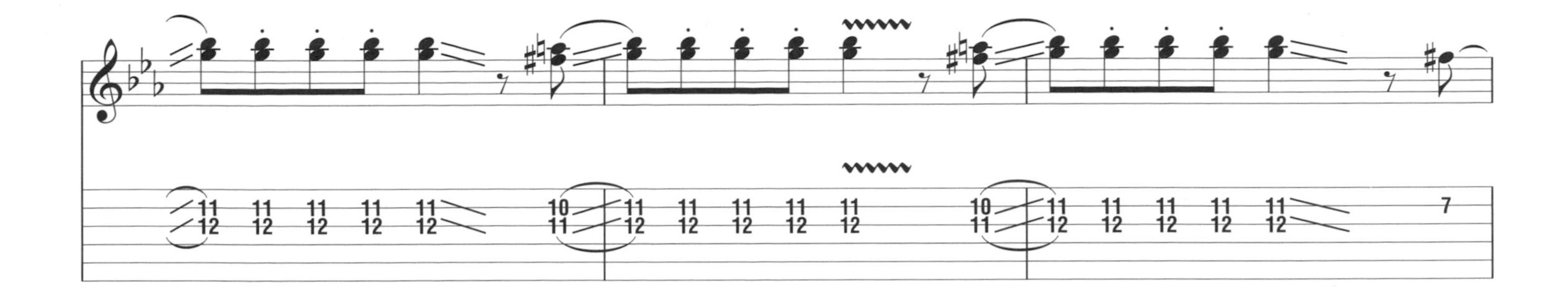

1/2
1/2

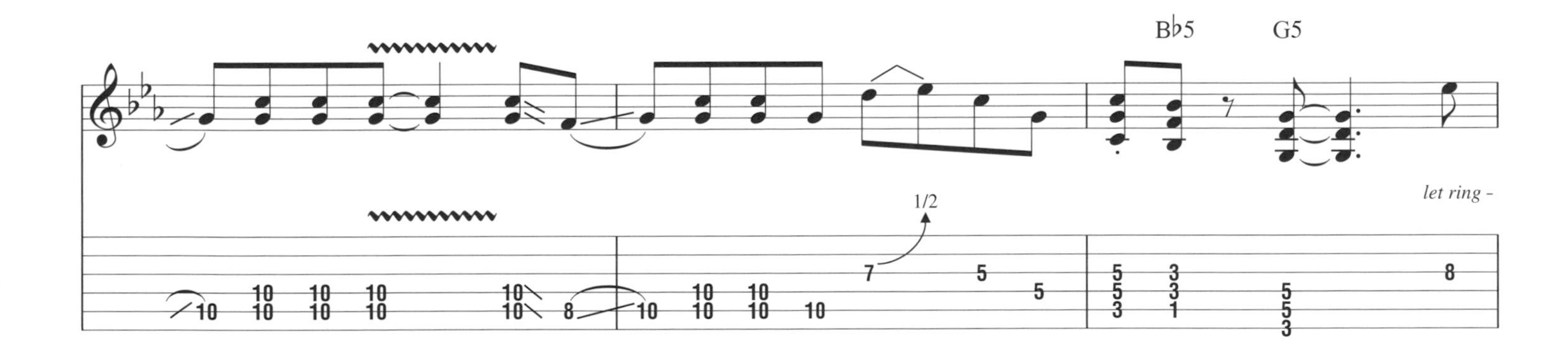
B♭5
G5
let ring
1/2

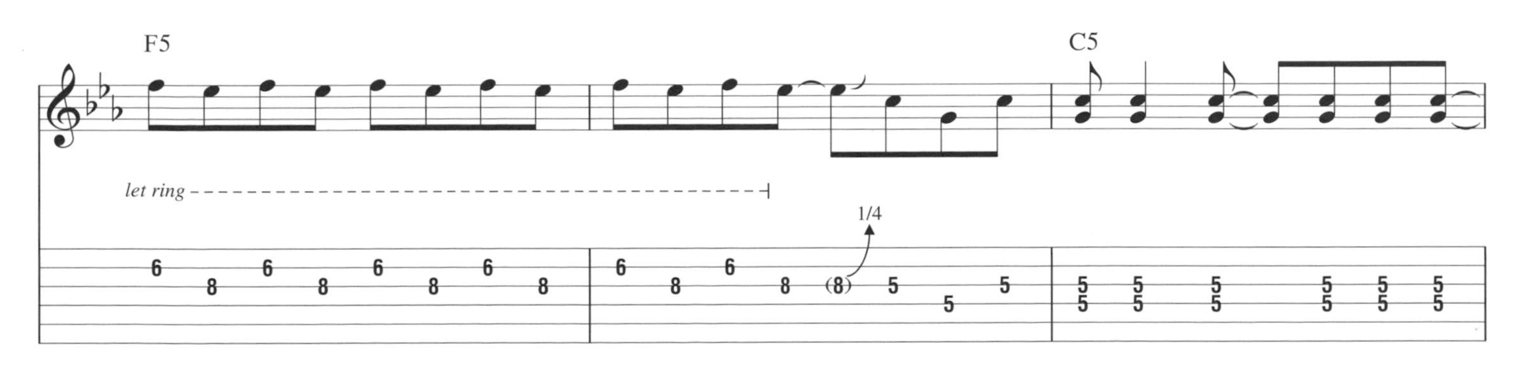
F5
C5
let ring
1/4

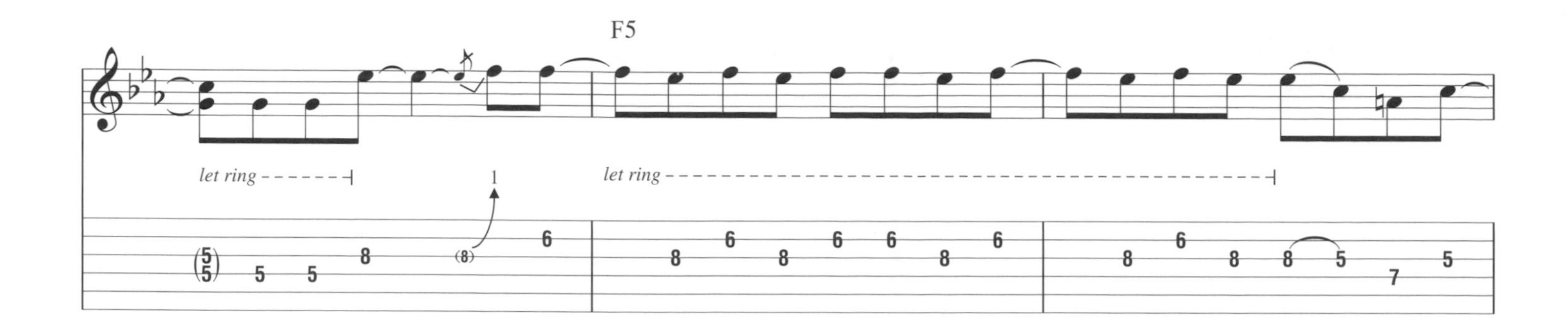
F5
let ring
1
let ring

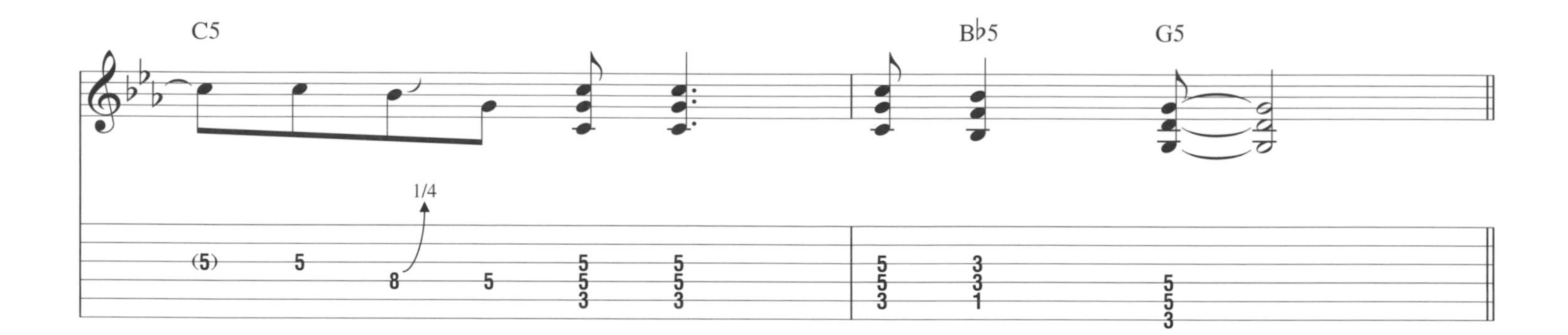
C5
B♭5
G5
1/4

Interlude
Cm7
How, how.
P.M.
P.M.
P.M.
P.M.
let ring

3rd time, D.S. al Coda 2
Play 3 times
P.M.
P.M.
P.M.
let ring

Coda 2
Chorus
G5
F5
G5
B♭5
C5
They come run - nin' just as fast as they can, 'cause
ev - 'ry girl's cra - zy 'bout a sharp dressed man.
E♭5
B♭5
Outro-Guitar Solo
C5
P.H.
P.H.
P.M.
P.H.

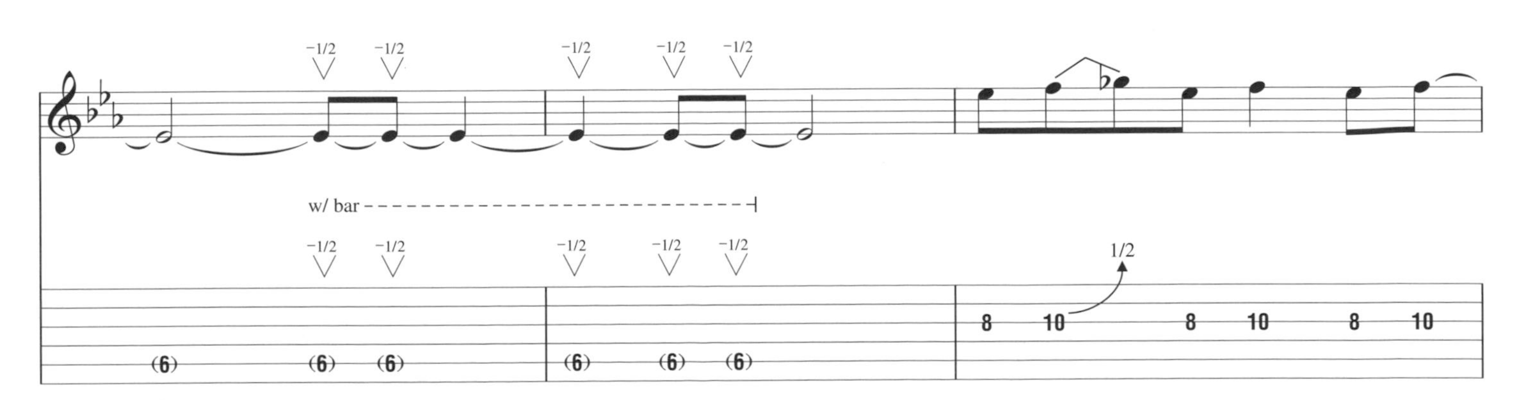
w/ bar

P.M.

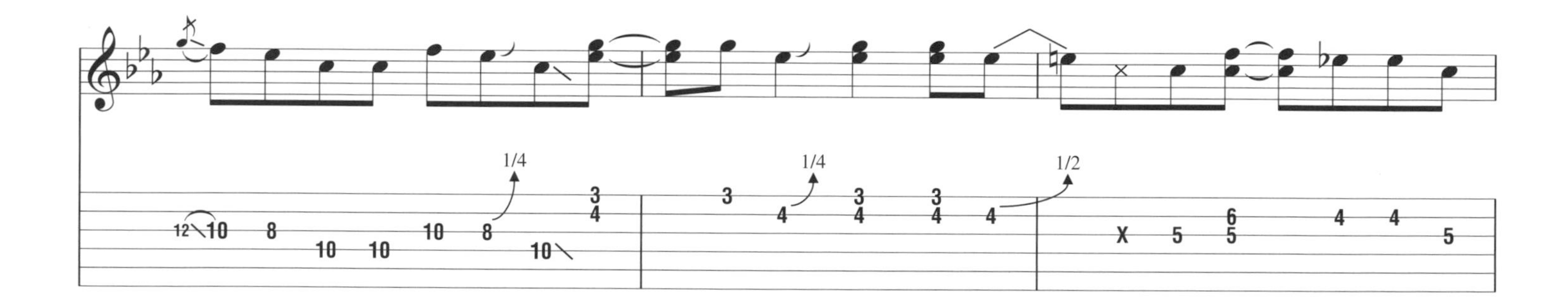

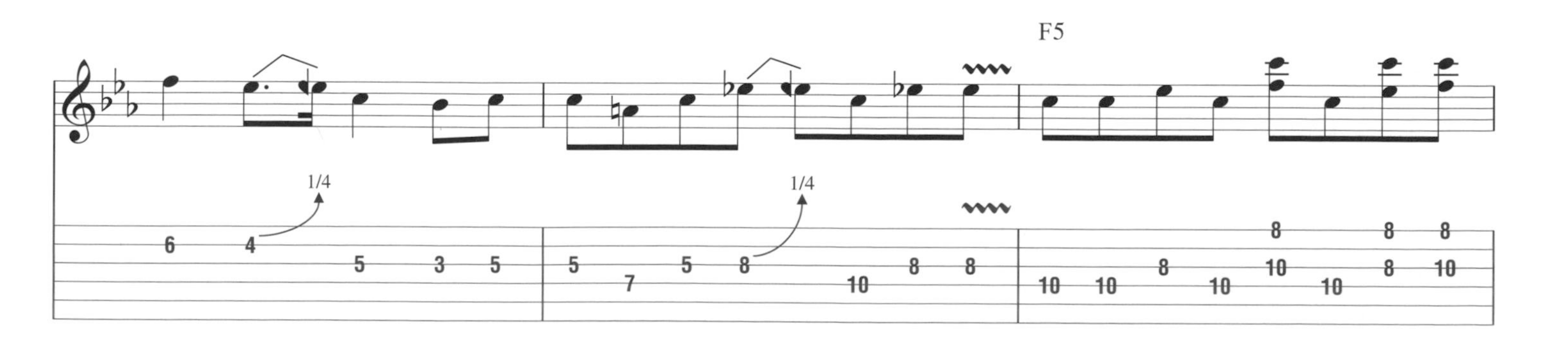
F5

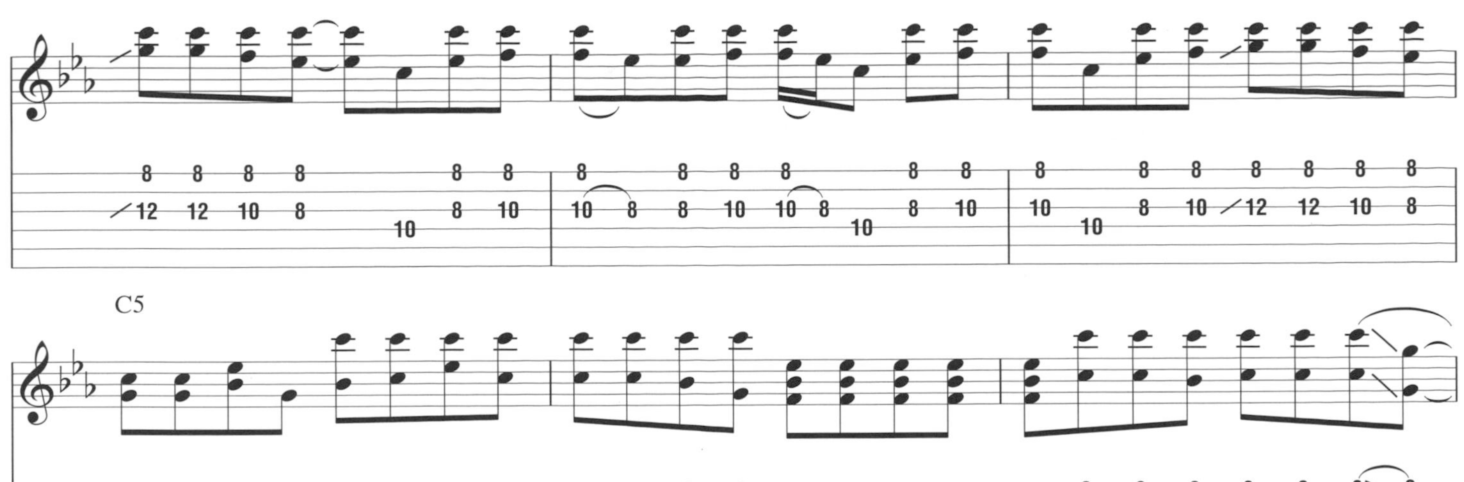

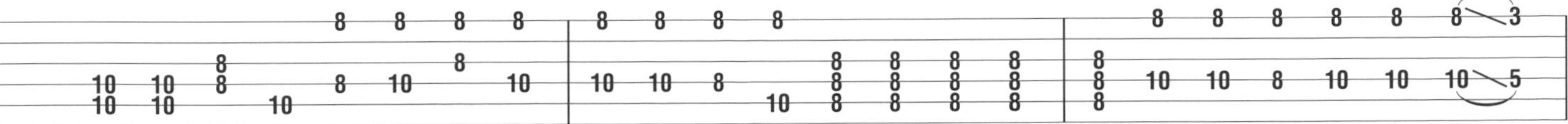

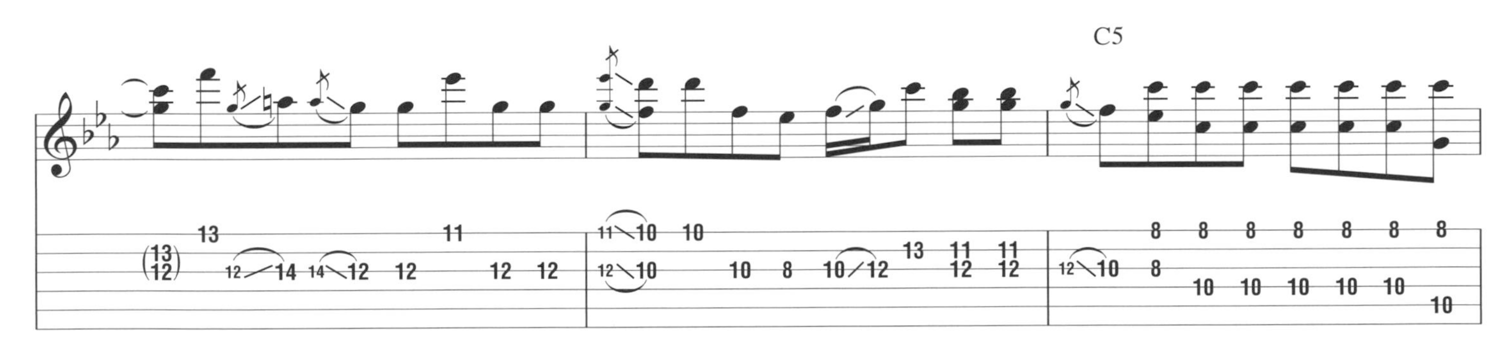

Additional Lyrics

2. Gold watch, diamond ring,
   I ain't missin' not a single thing.
   Cuff links, stick pin,
   When I step out I'm gonna do you in.

3. Top coat, top hat,
   An' I don't worry 'cause my wallet's fat.
   Black shades, white gloves,
   Lookin' sharp, lookin' for love.

Stages

Words and Music by Billy F Gibbons, Dusty Hill and Frank Lee Beard

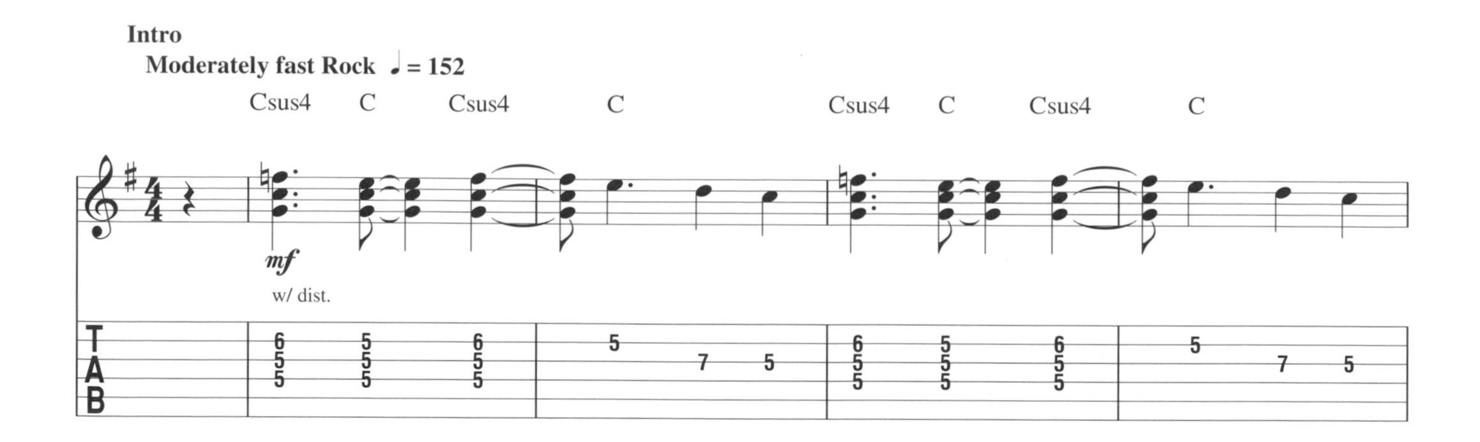

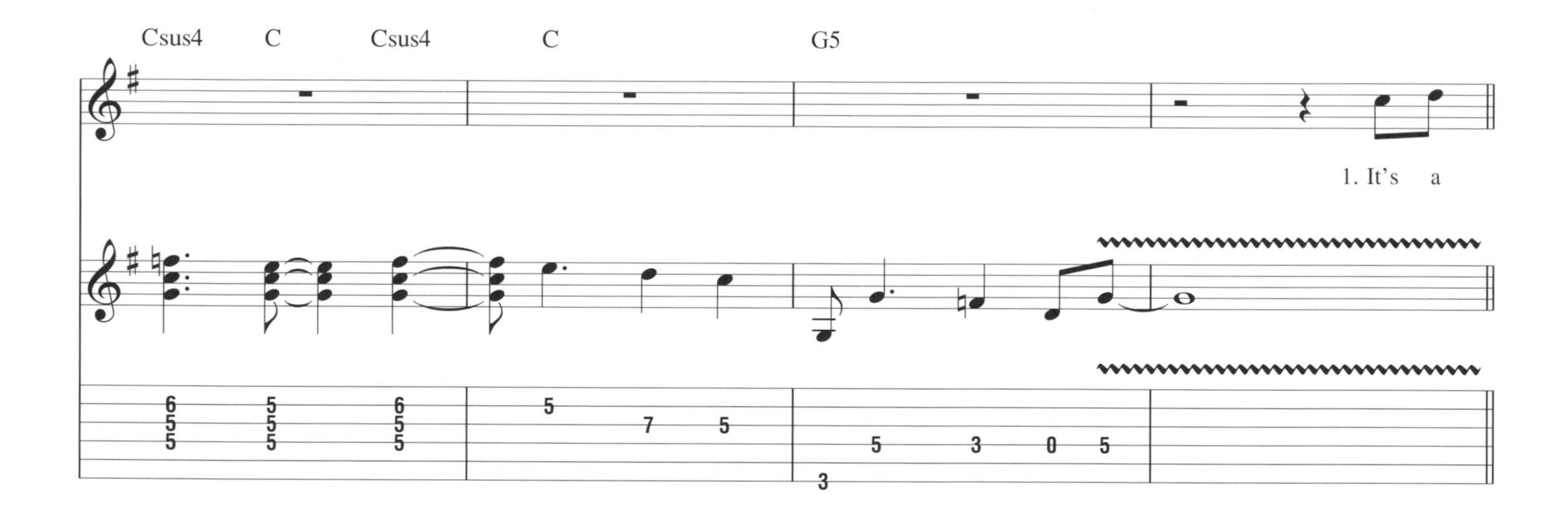

Em7
D/E
Em7
D/E
ain't got a sin - gle thing to do.

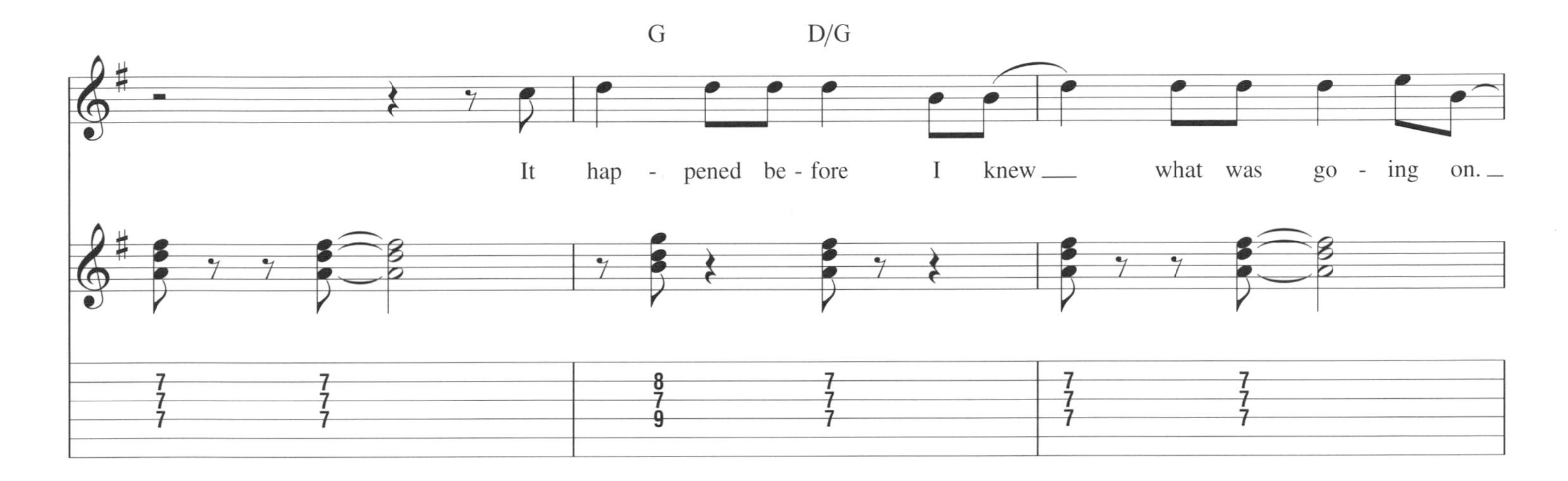
G
D/G
It hap - pened be - fore I knew what was go - ing on.

G
D/G
Em7
D/E
I fell out and knew

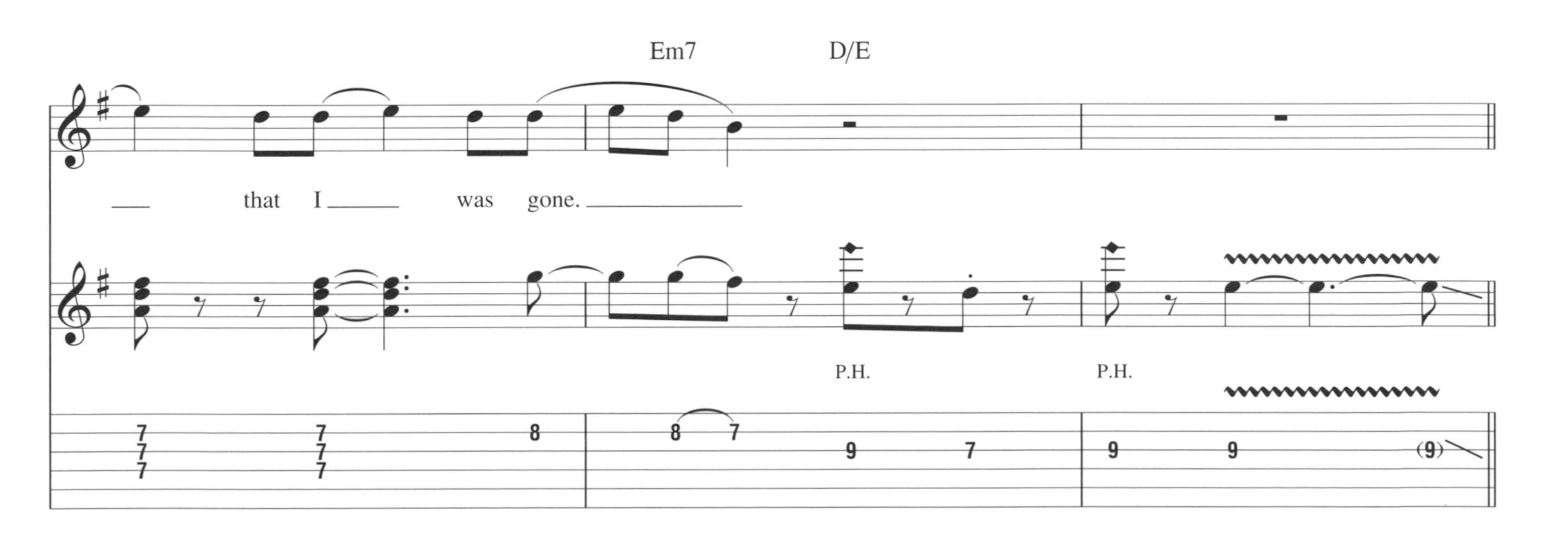
Em7
D/E
that I was gone.
P.H.
P.H.

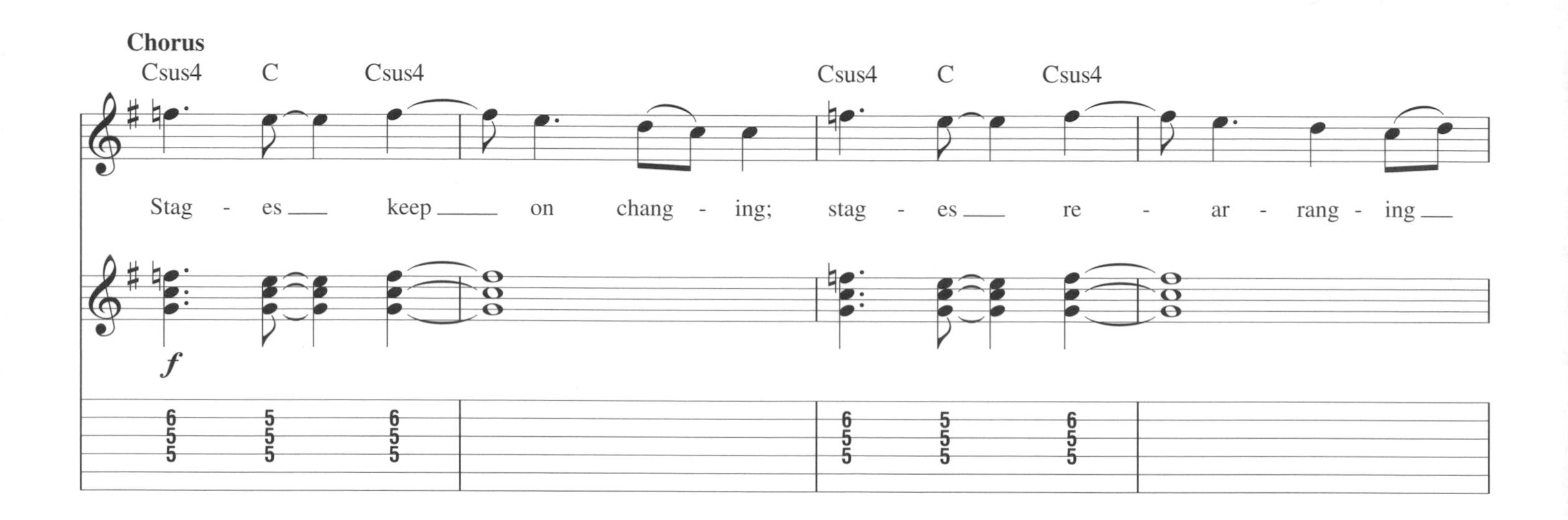
Chorus
Csus4
C
Csus4
Csus4
C
Csus4
Stag - es keep on chang - ing; stag - es re - ar - rang - ing

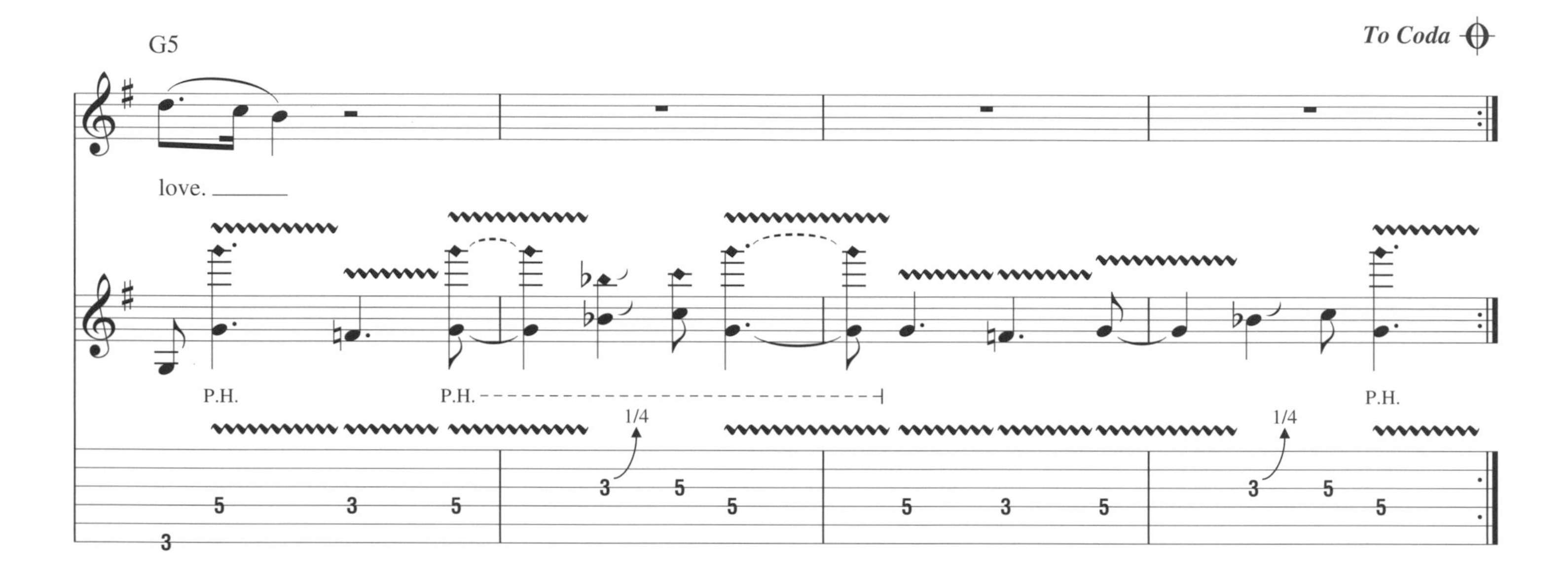
G5
To Coda
love.
P.H.
P.H.
P.H.
1/4
1/4

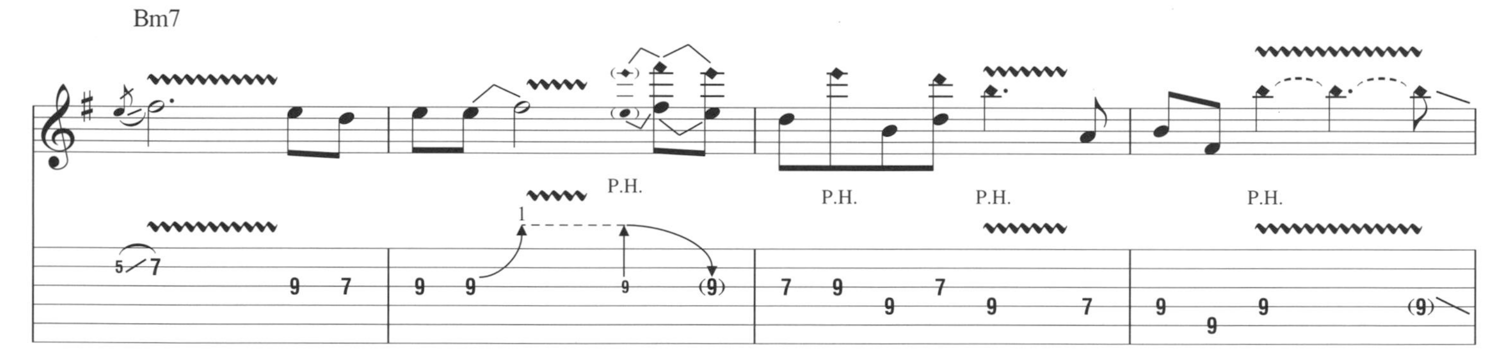
Guitar Solo
Bm7
P.H.
P.H.
P.H.
P.H.

A
P.H.
P.H.
P.H.
1/4
1/2
1/2

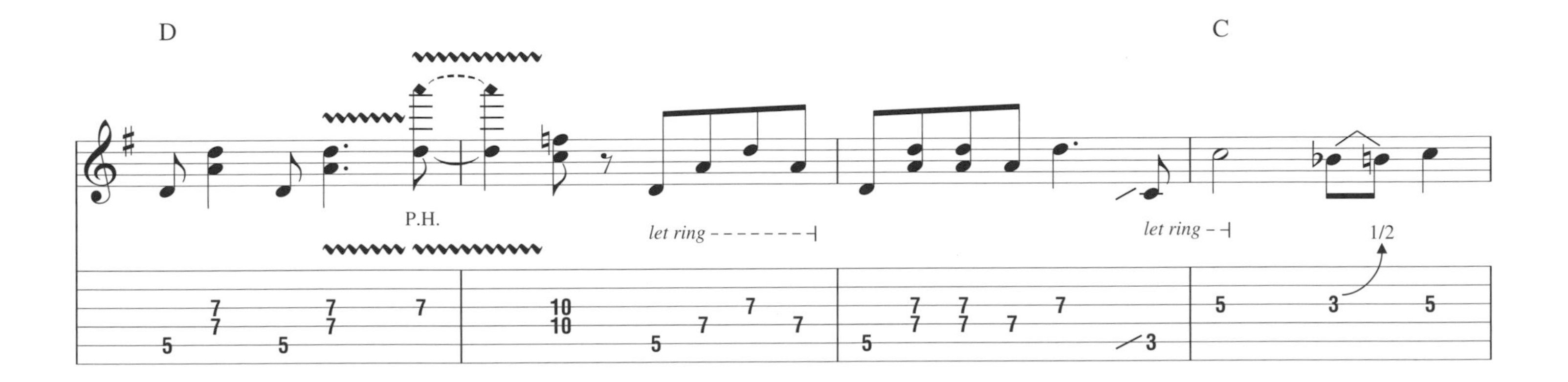

Coda

Outro-Guitar Solo

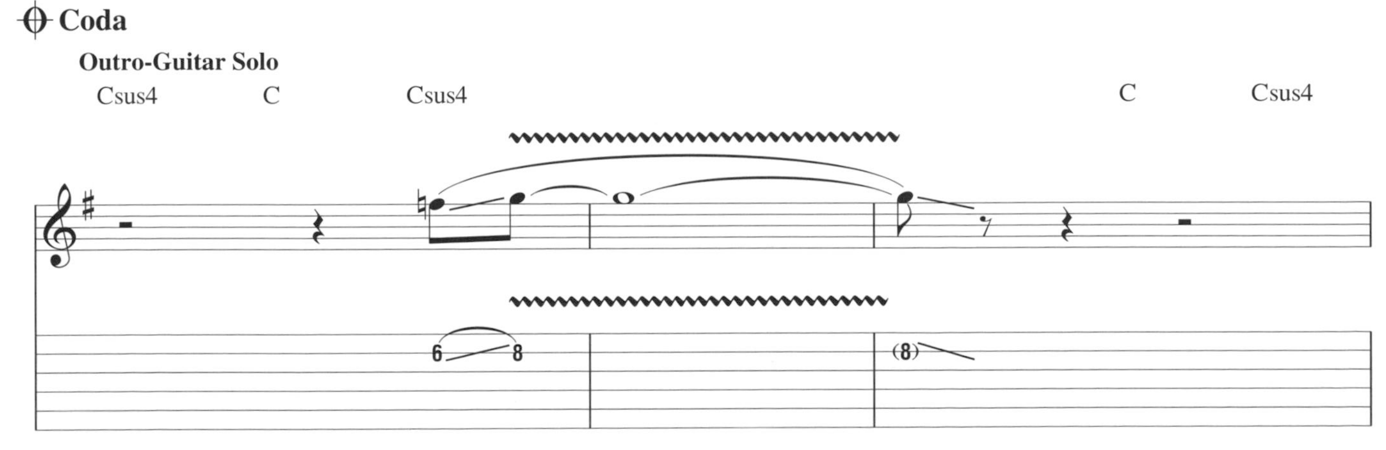

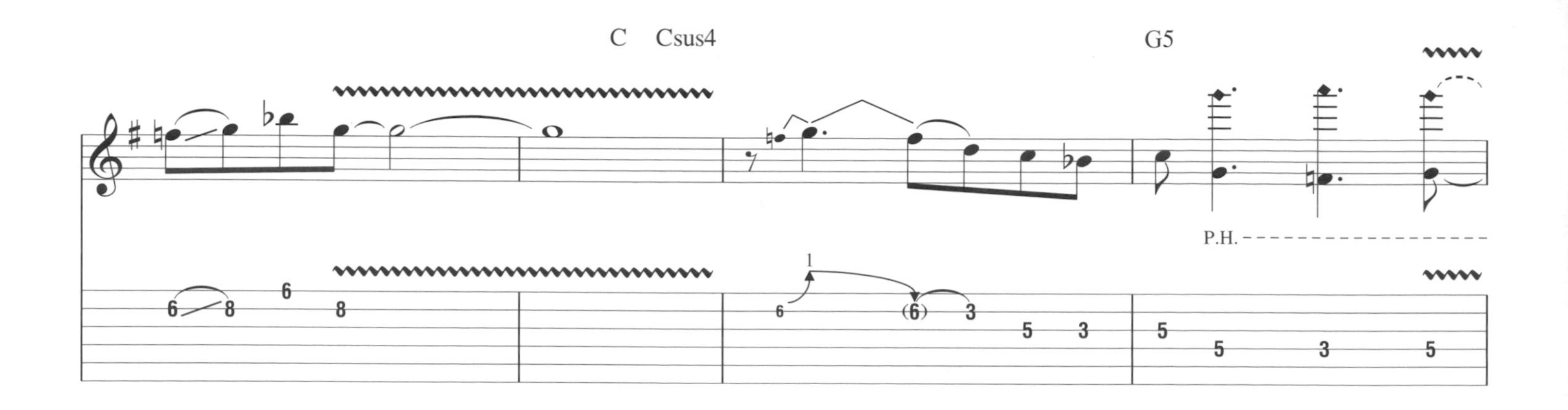
C Csus4
G5
P.H.

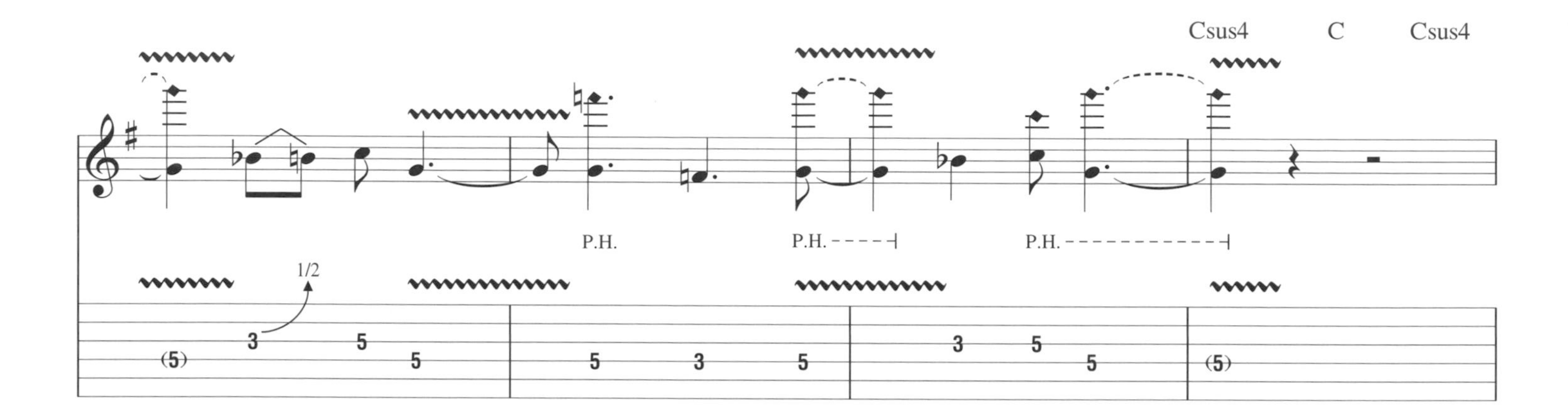
Csus4 C Csus4
P.H.
P.H.
P.H.

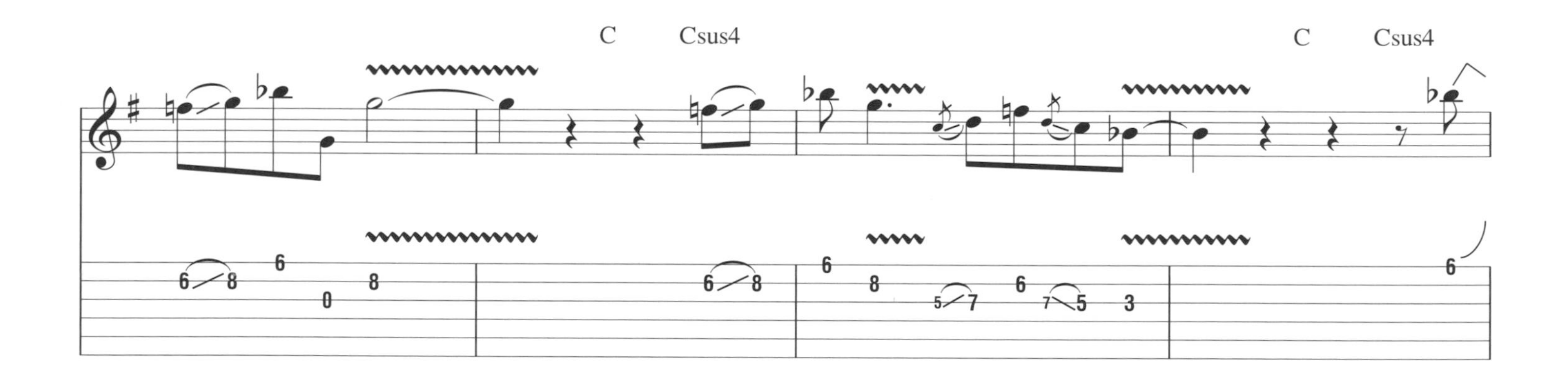
C Csus4
C Csus4

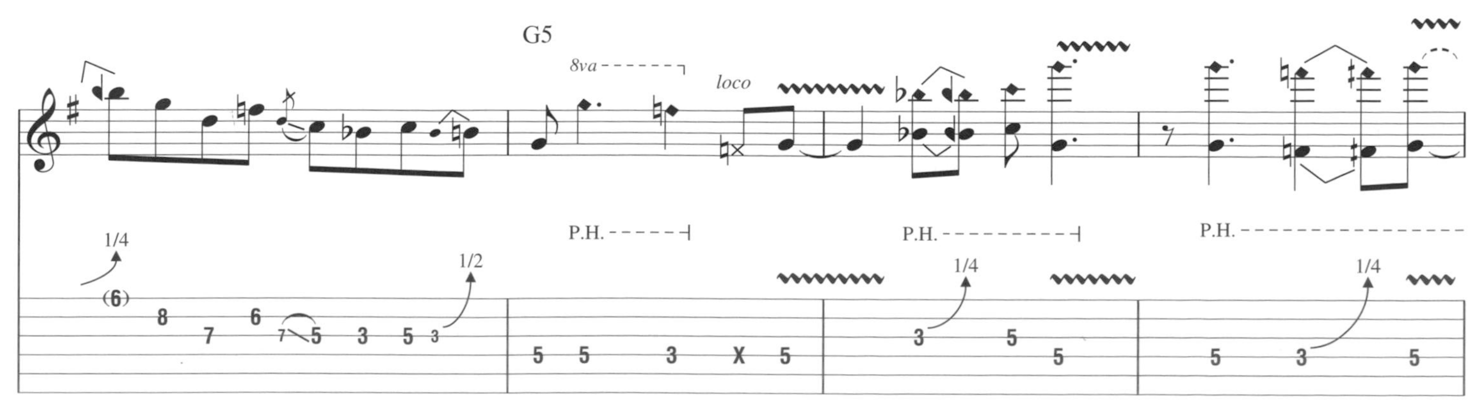
G5
8va
loco
P.H.
P.H.
P.H.

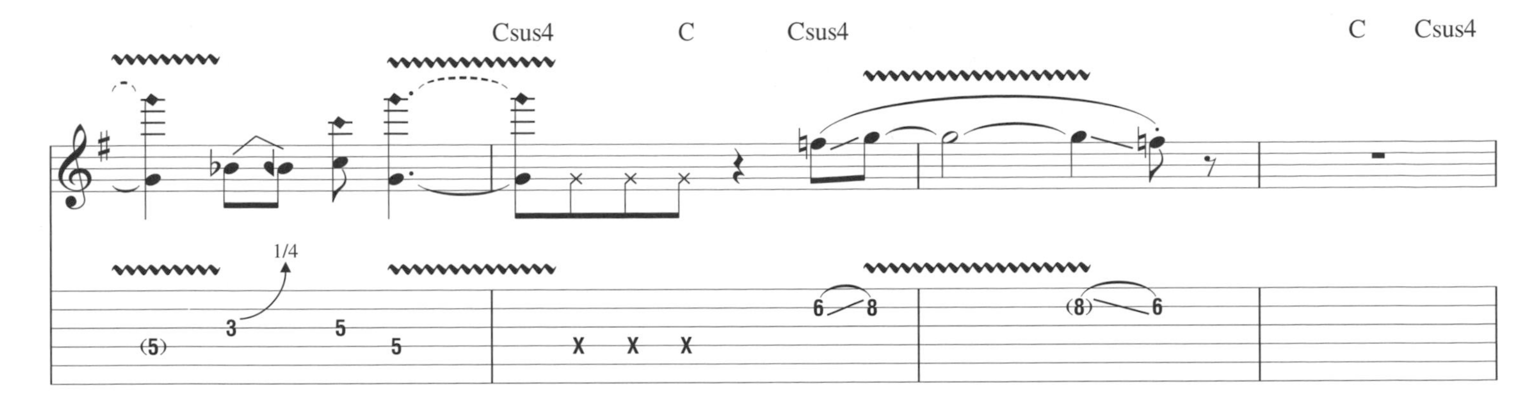

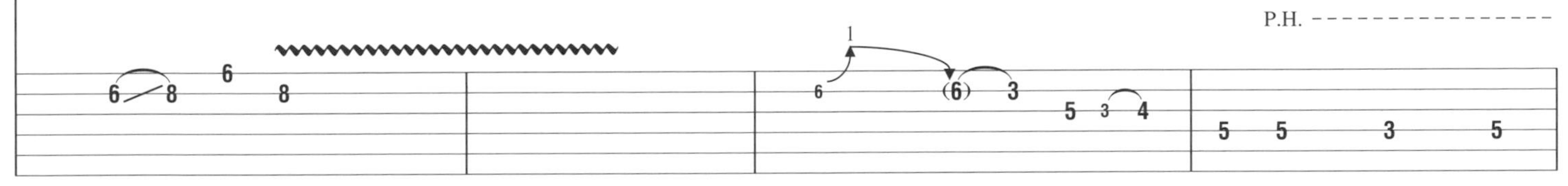

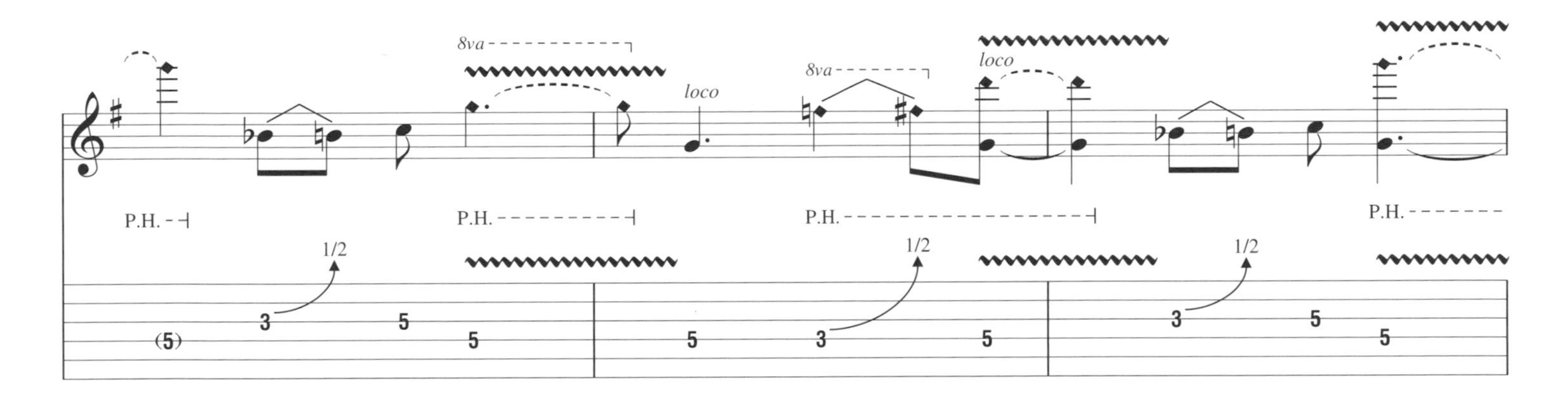

Additional Lyrics

2. Then you left me standing all alone.
   I couldn't even get you on the phone.
   Were you just confused and didn't know
   If you should stay or if you had to go?

3. Now you're back and say you're gonna stay.
   I wouldn't have it any other way.
   Tell me it's for real and let me know;
   Why does lovin' have to come and go?

Tube Snake Boogie

Words and Music by Billy F Gibbons, Dusty Hill and Frank Lee Beard

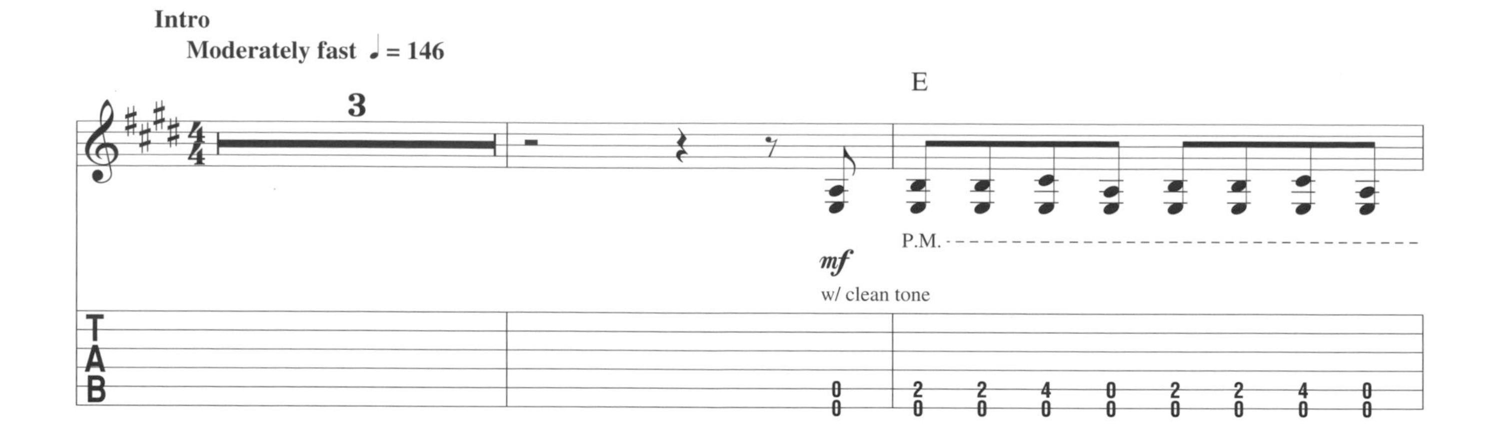

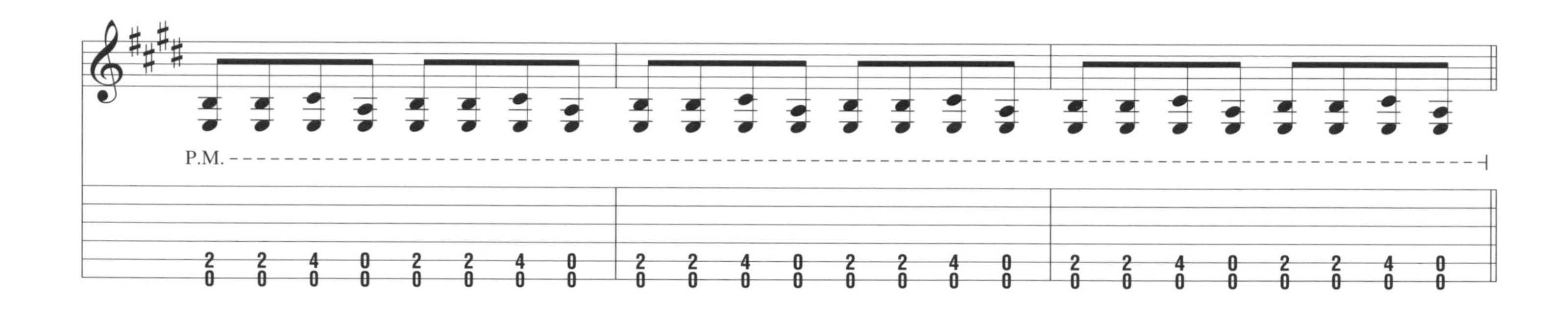

B7
1/2
let ring

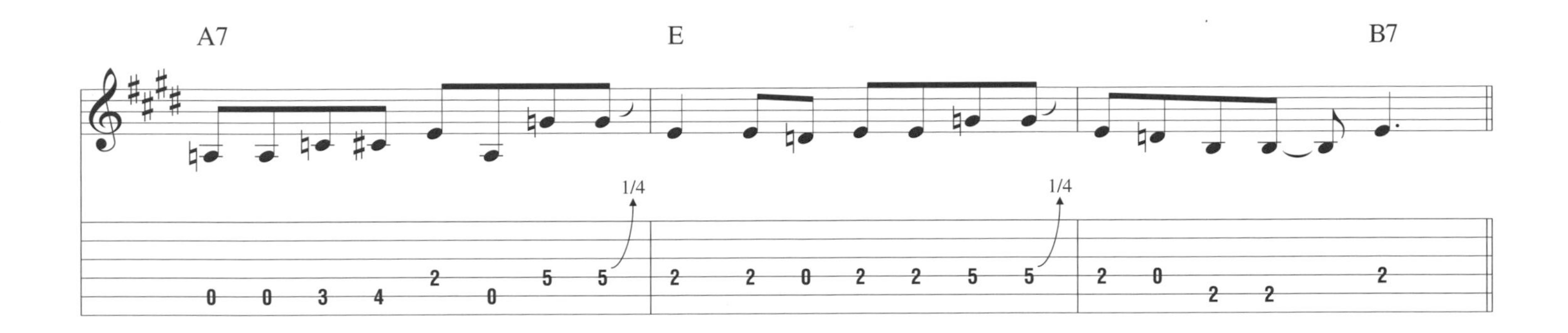
A7
E
B7
1/4
1/4

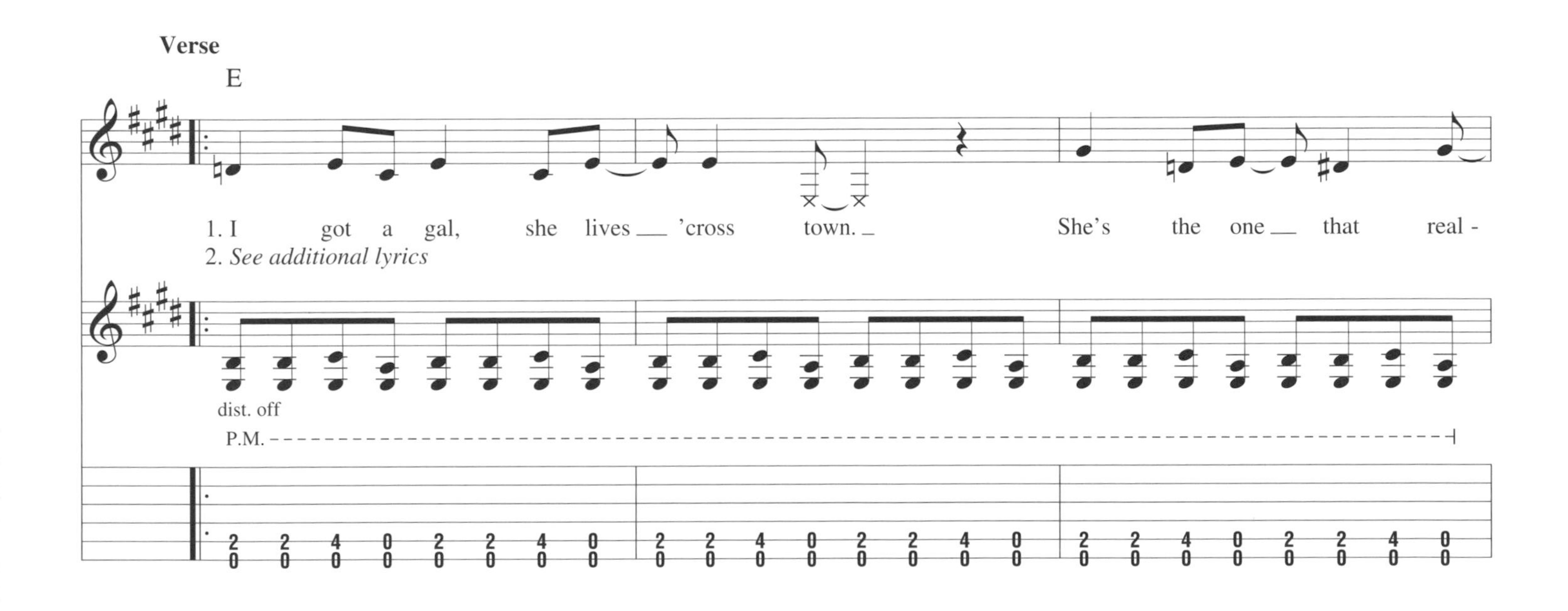
Verse
E
1. I got a gal, she lives 'cross town. She's the one that real-
2. See additional lyrics
dist. off
P.M.

N.C.
A
Asus2/4
A
Asus2/4
A
-ly gets down when she boo-gie, she do the

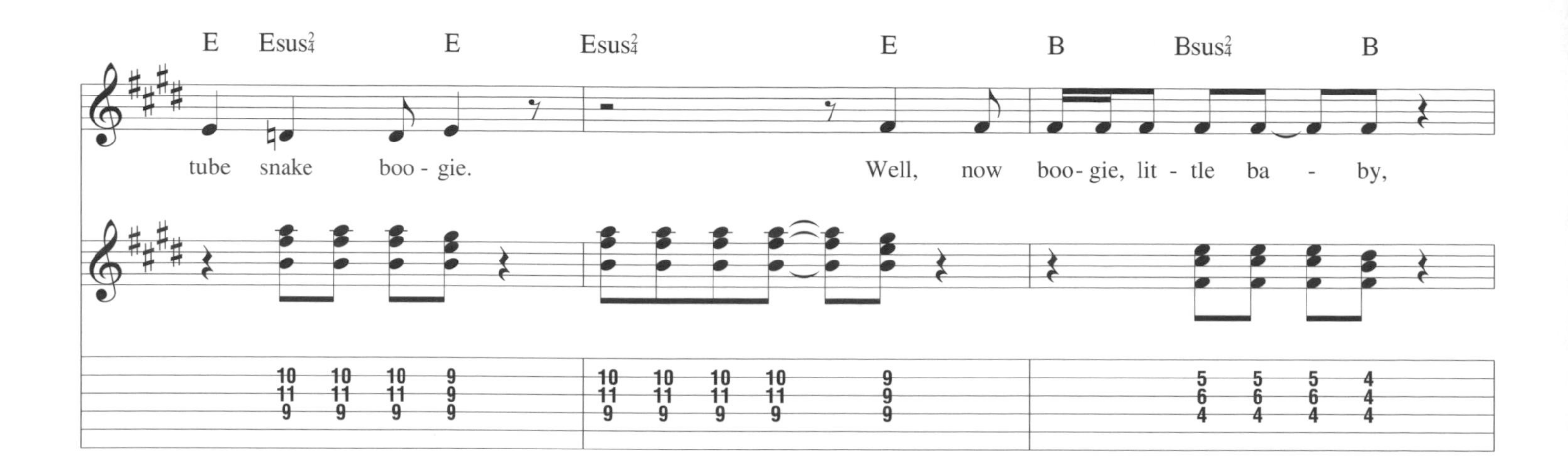
E Esus2/4 E Esus2/4 E B Bsus2/4 B
tube snake boo - gie. Well, now boo- gie, lit - tle ba - by,

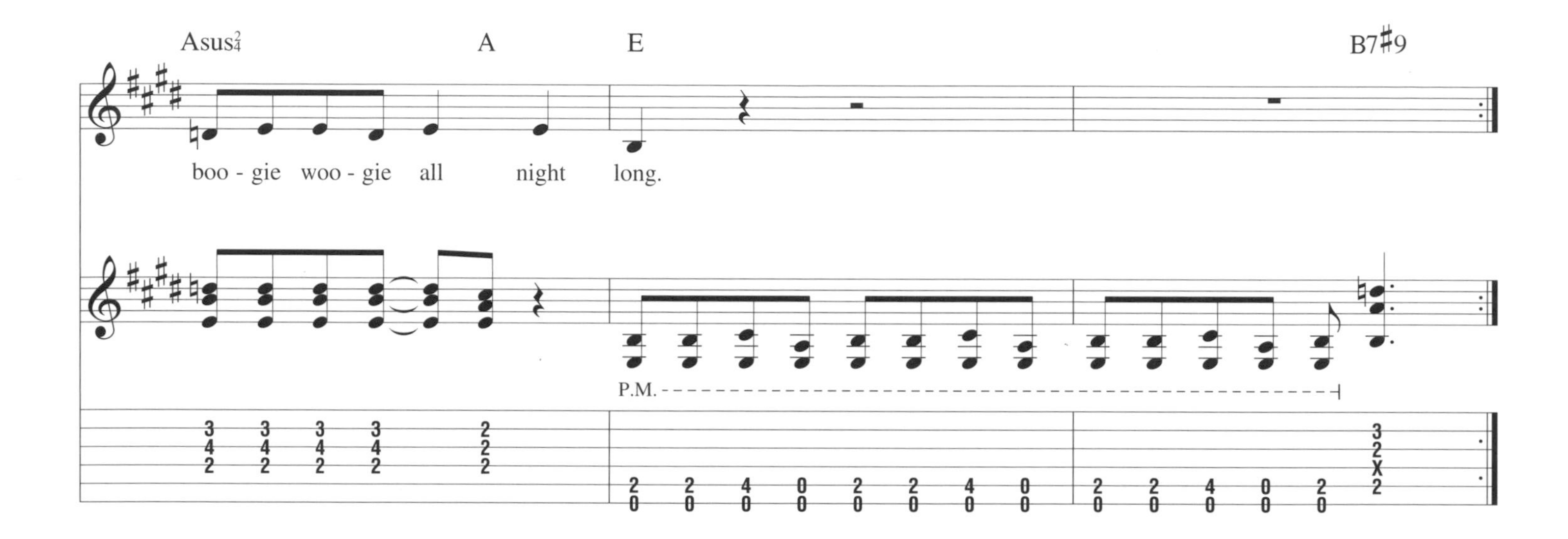
Asus2/4 A E B7#9
boo - gie woo - gie all night long.
P.M.

Guitar Solo

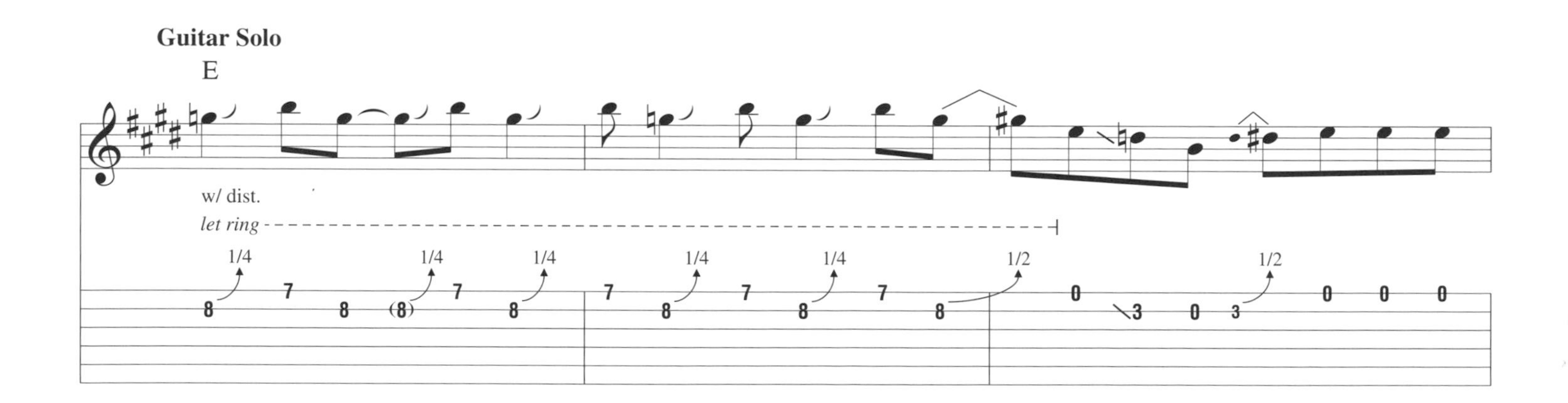
E
w/ dist.
let ring

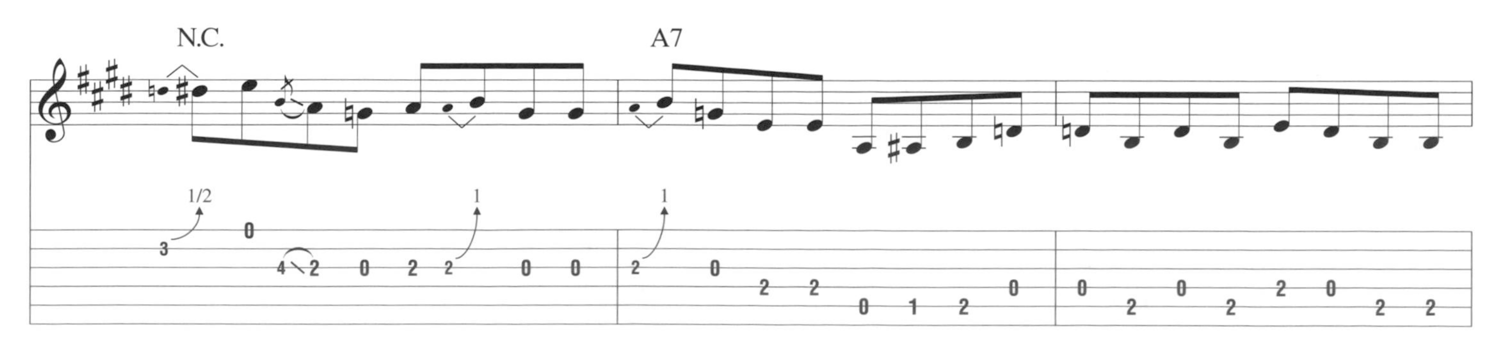
N.C. A7

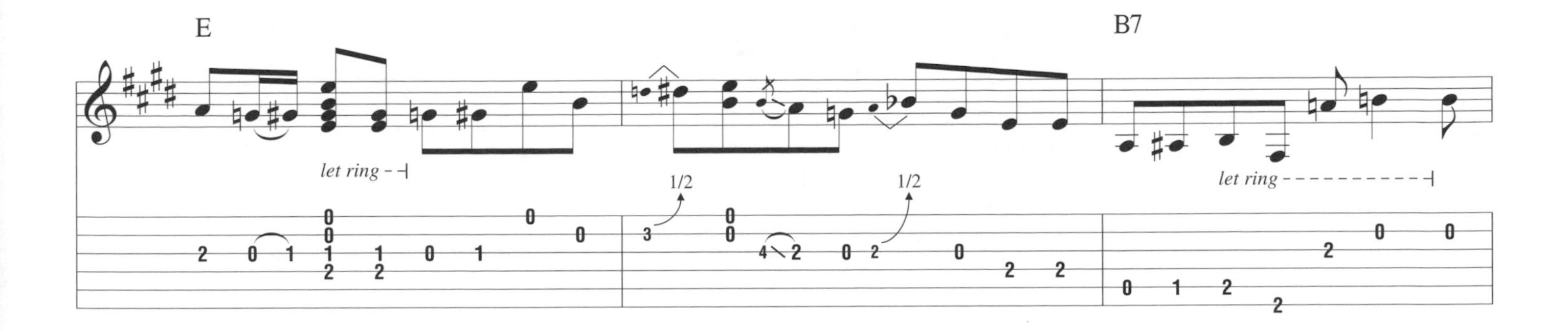
E
B7
let ring
1/2
1/2
let ring

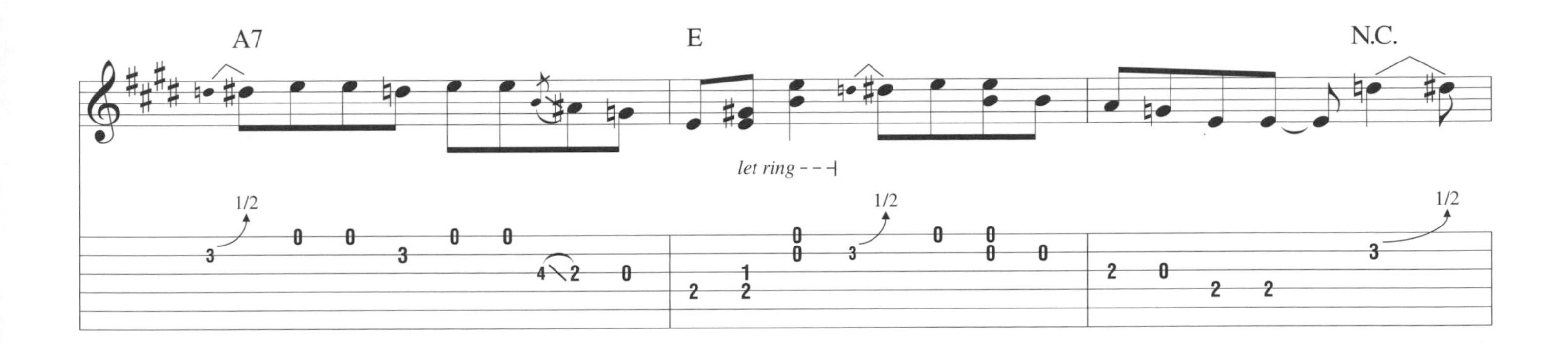
A7
E
N.C.
let ring
1/2
1/2
1/2

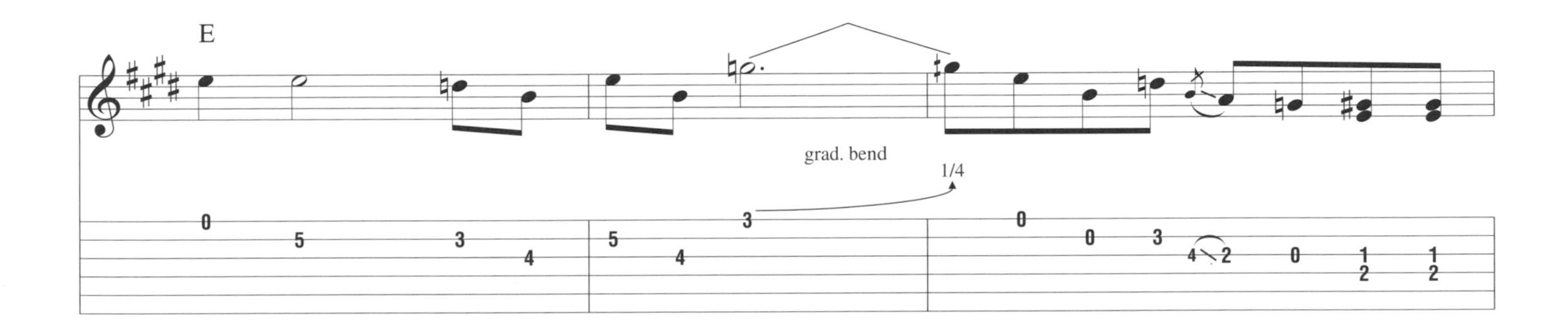
E
grad. bend
1/4

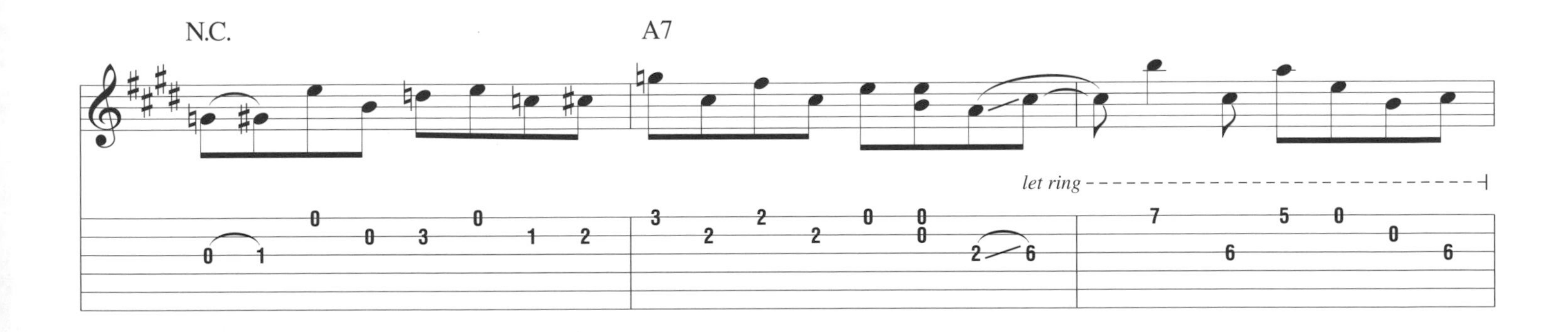
N.C.
A7
let ring

E
B7
1

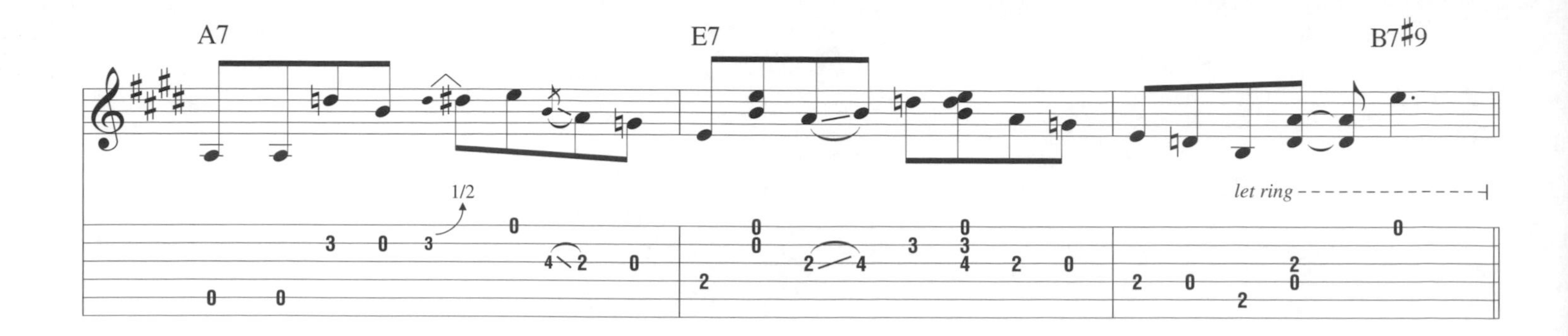
A7
E7
B7♯9
1/2
let ring

Verse
Gtr. tacet
N.C.
3. I got a gal, she lives ___ on the hill. ___ She won't do it but her

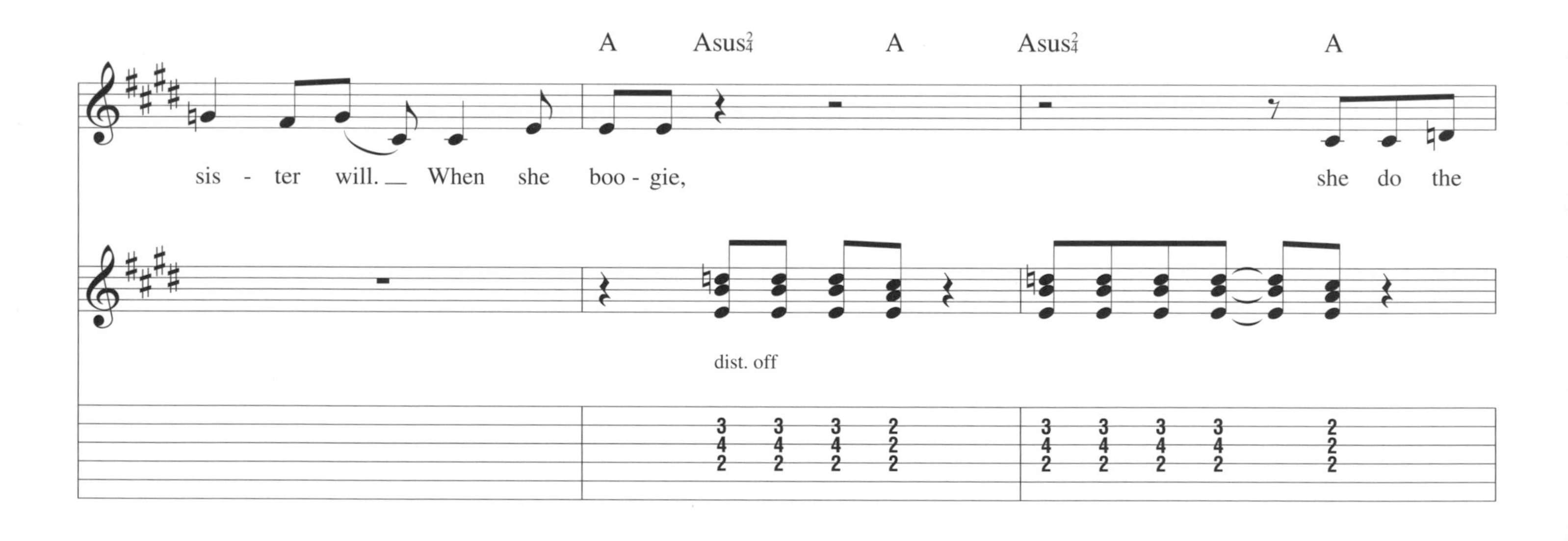
A Asus2/4 A Asus2/4 A
sis - ter will. ___ When she boo - gie, she do the
dist. off

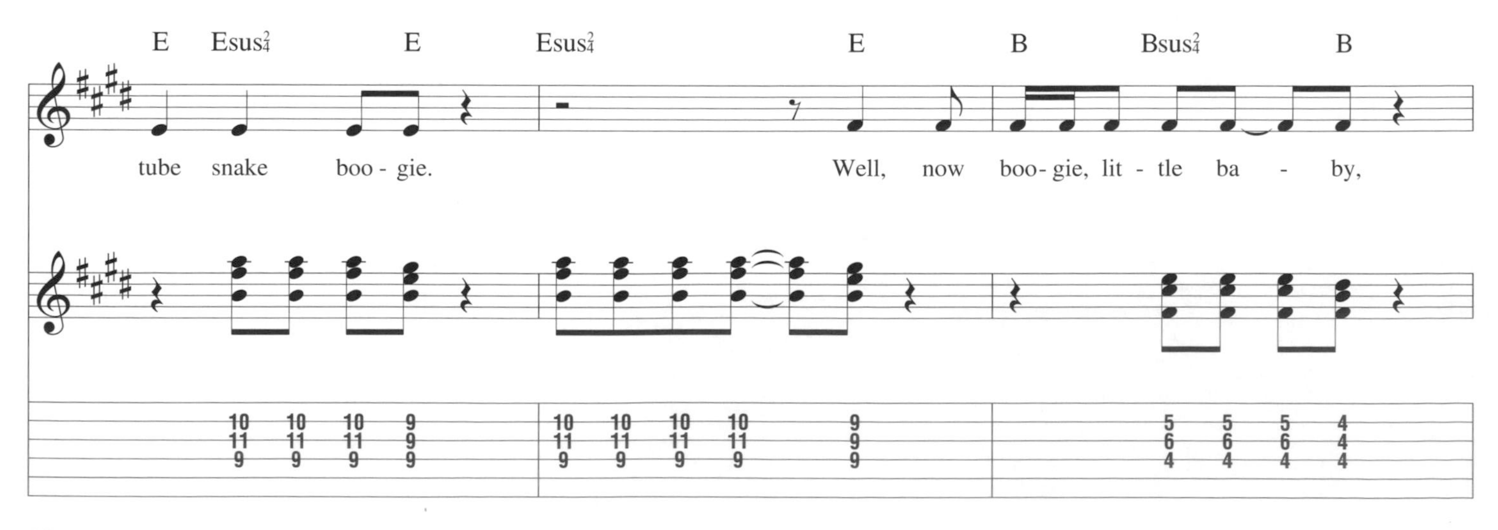
E Esus2/4 E Esus2/4 E B Bsus2/4 B
tube snake boo - gie. Well, now boo - gie, lit - tle ba - by,

Outro-Guitar Solo

E

w/ dist.

let ring

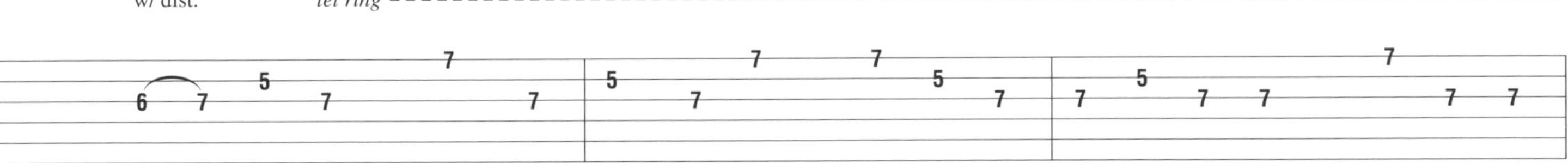

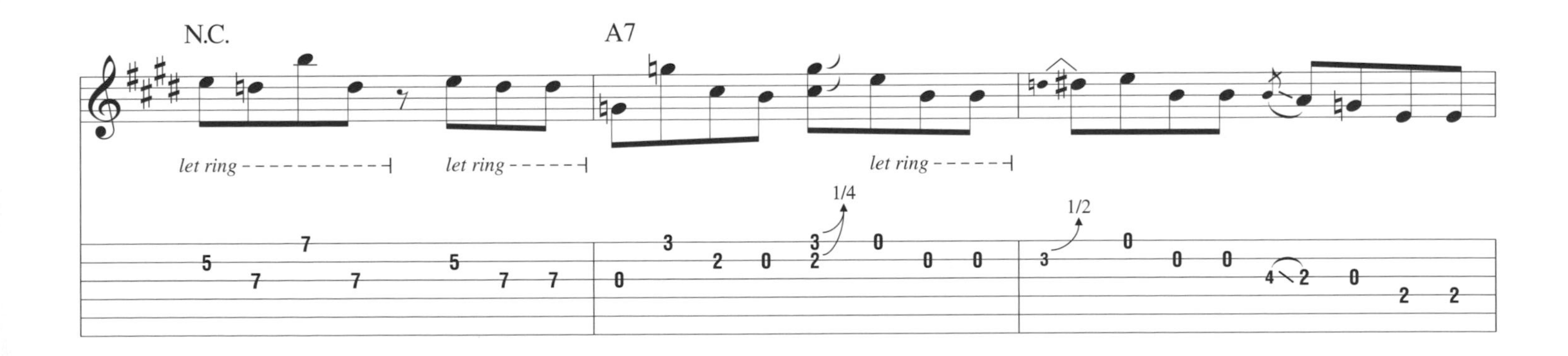

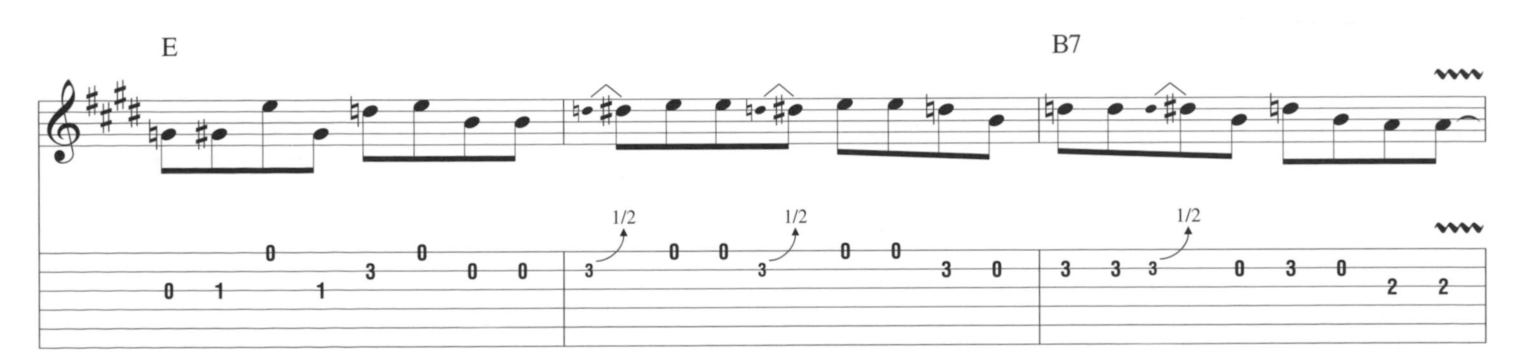

A7
E
B7♯9

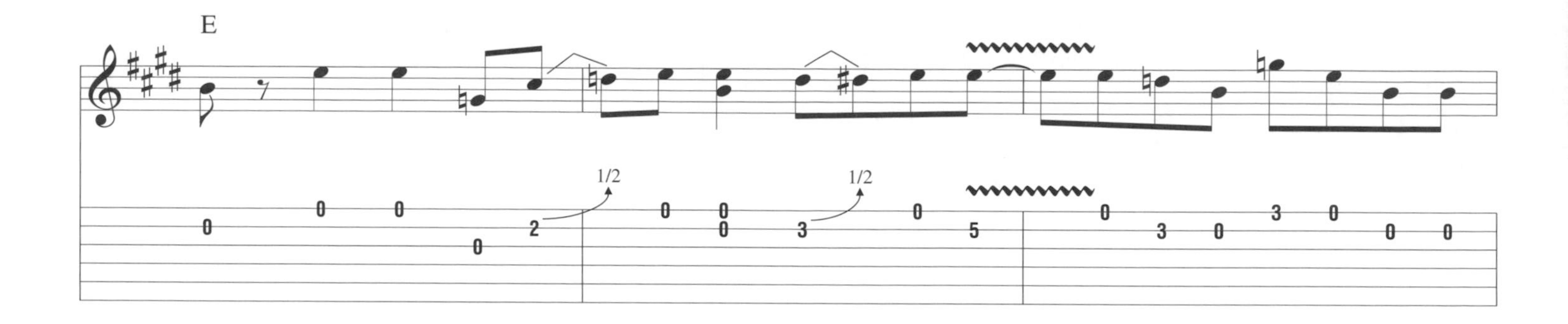
E
1/2
1/2

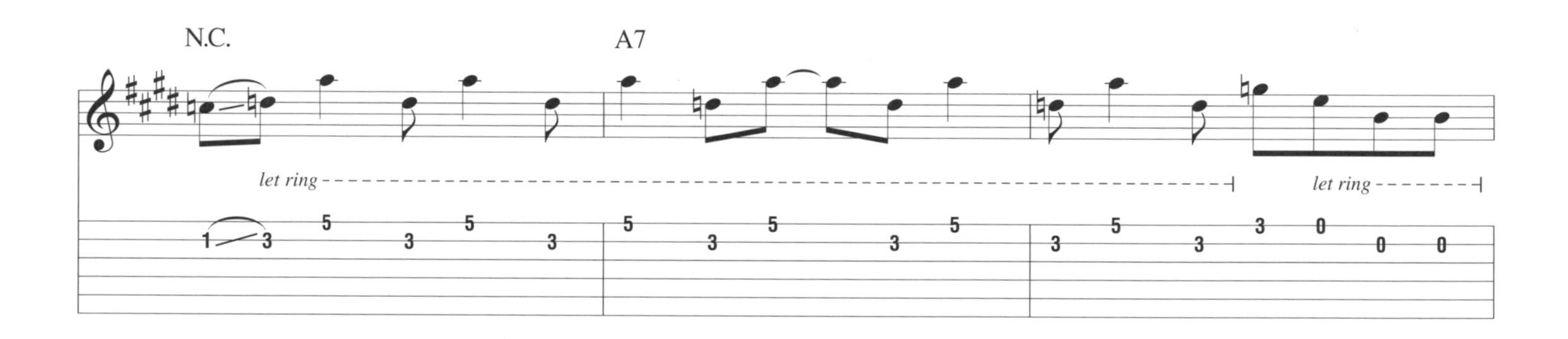
N.C.
A7
let ring
let ring

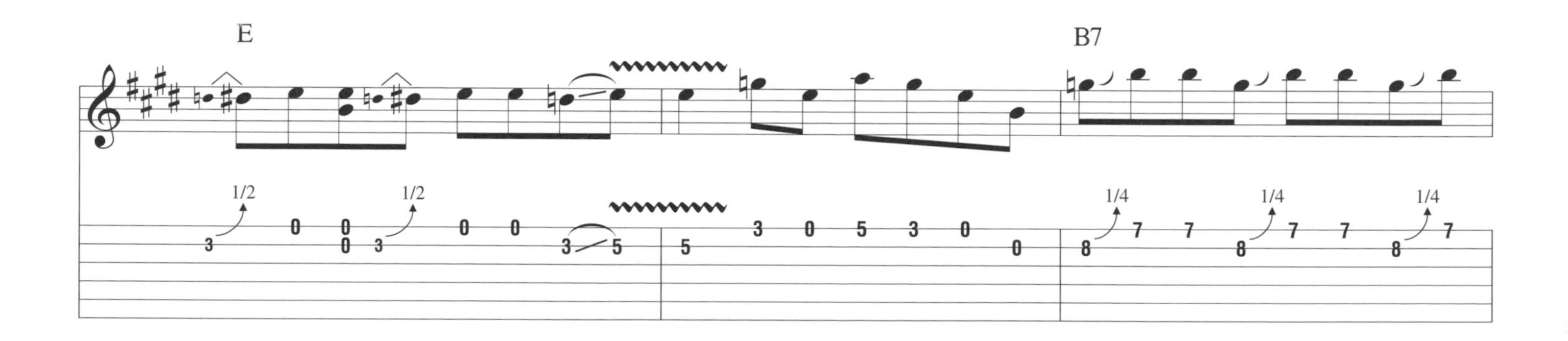
E
B7
1/2
1/2
1/4
1/4
1/4

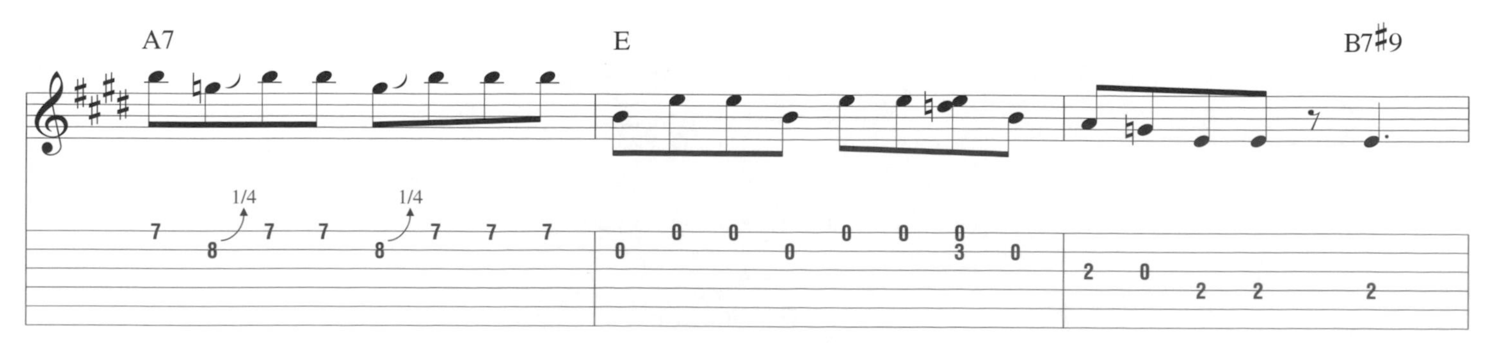
A7
E
B7♯9
1/4
1/4

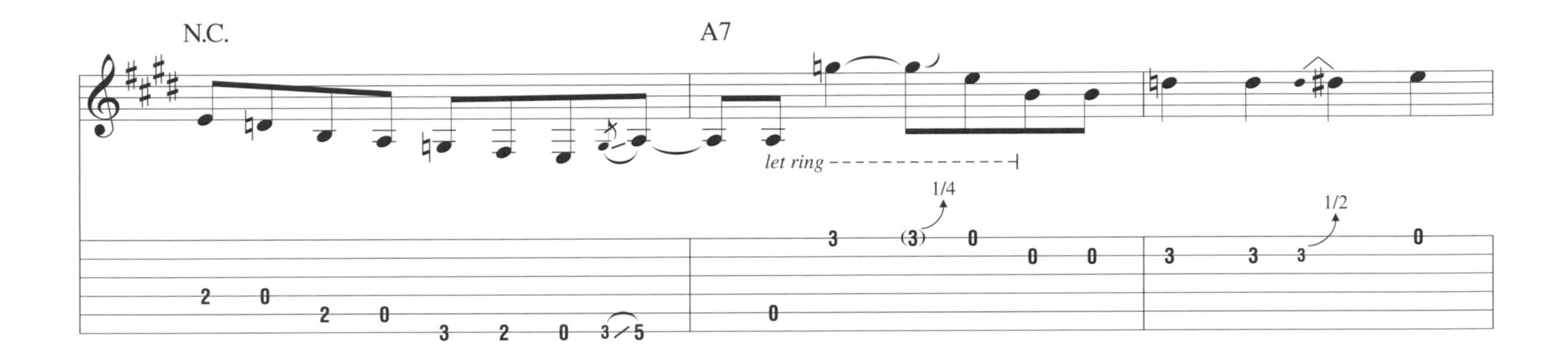

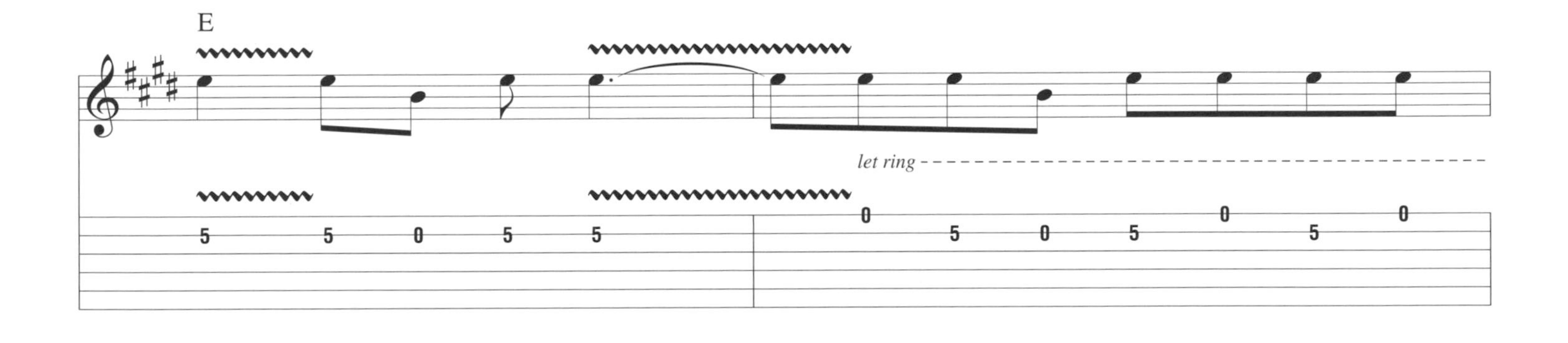

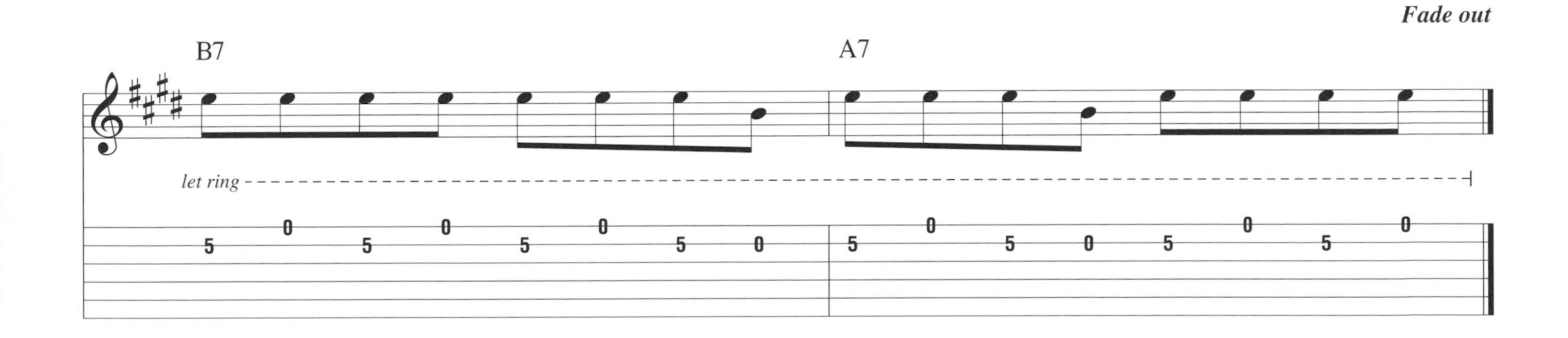

Additional Lyrics

2. I got a gal, she lives on the block.
   She's kinda funky with her pink and black socks.
   She like to boogie, she do the tube snake boogie.
   Well, now boogie woogie, baby, boogie woogie all night long.

Waitin' for the Bus

Words and Music by Billy F Gibbons and Dusty Hill

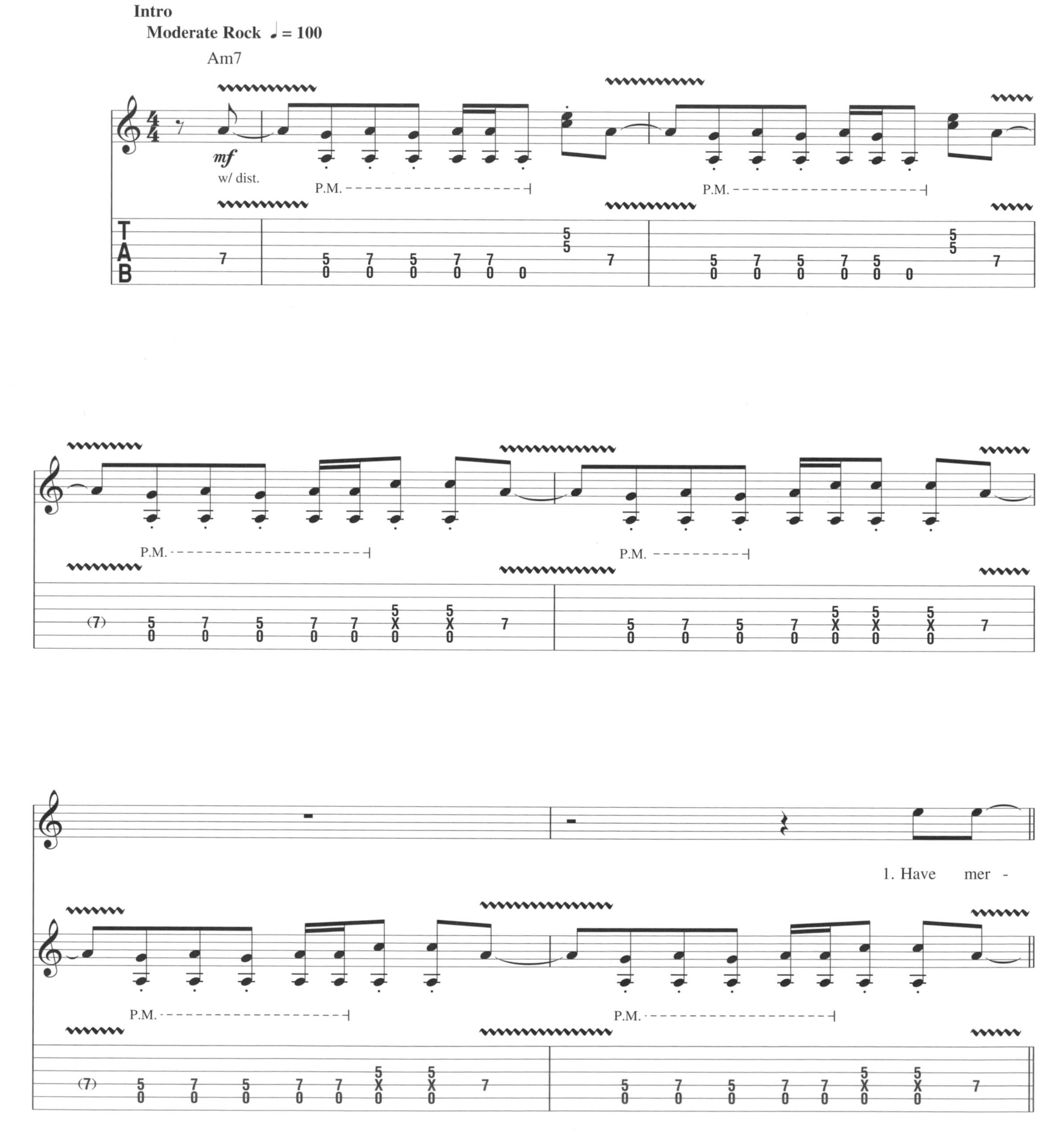

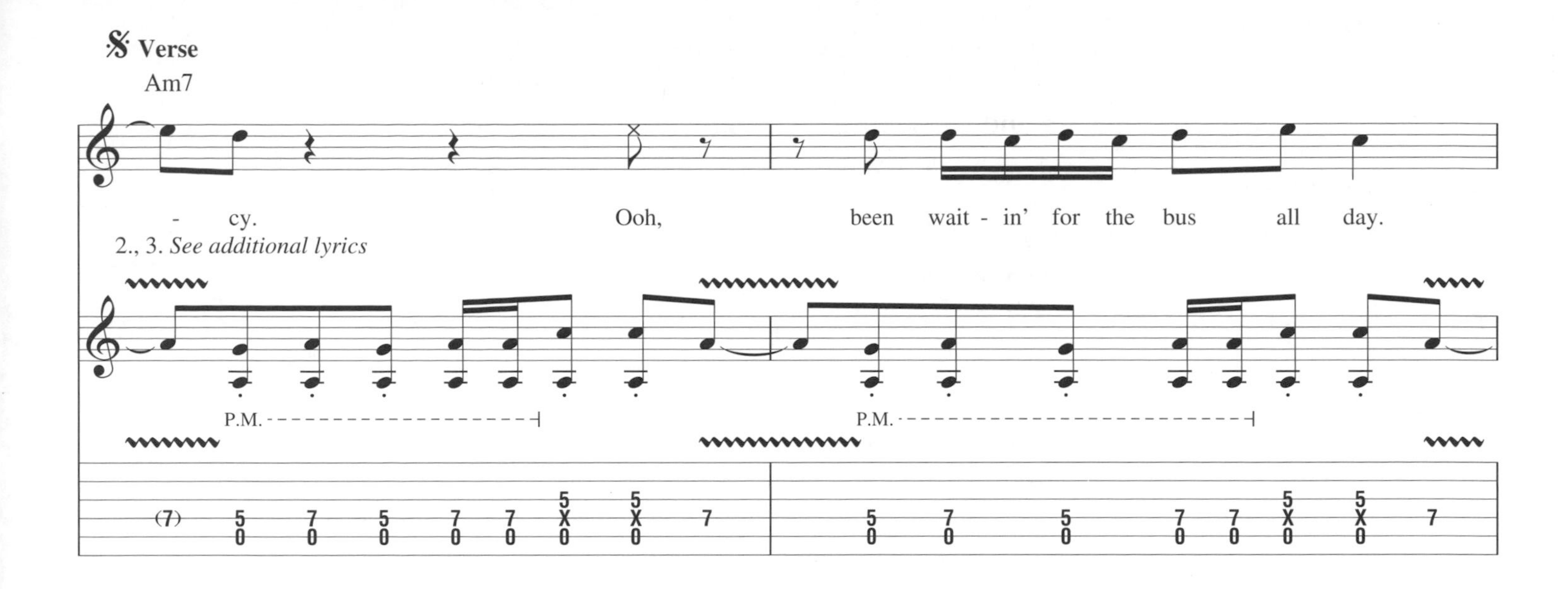
Verse
Am7
- cy. Ooh, been wait - in' for the bus all day.
2., 3. See additional lyrics
P.M.
P.M.

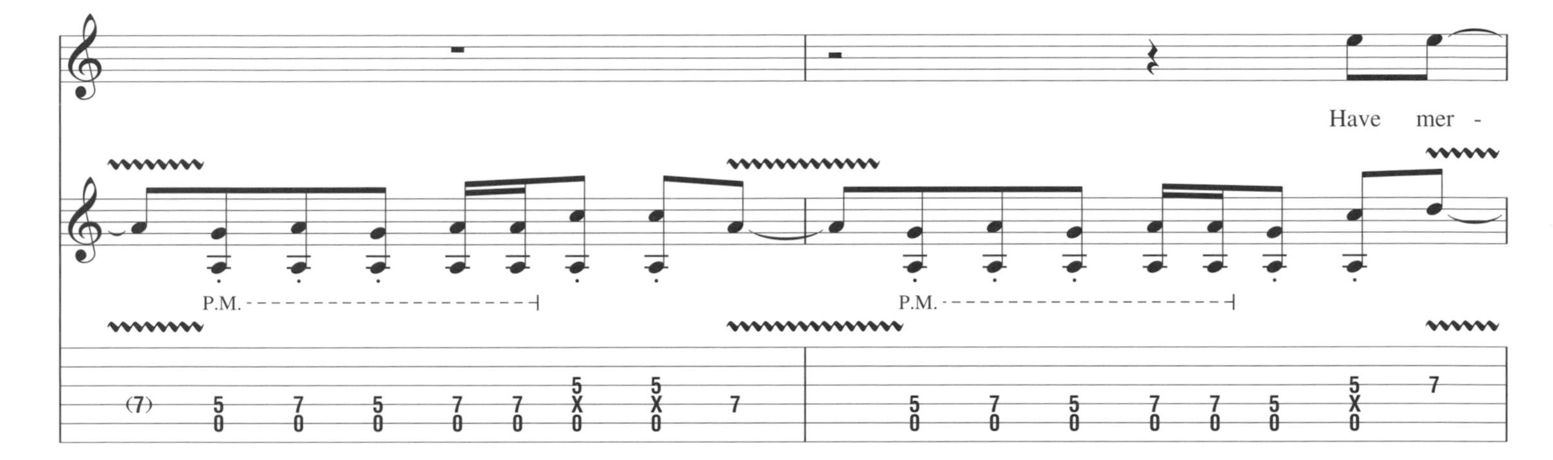
Have mer -
P.M.
P.M.

Dm7
- cy. Been wait - in' for the bus all day.
P.M.
P.M.
1/4
1/4

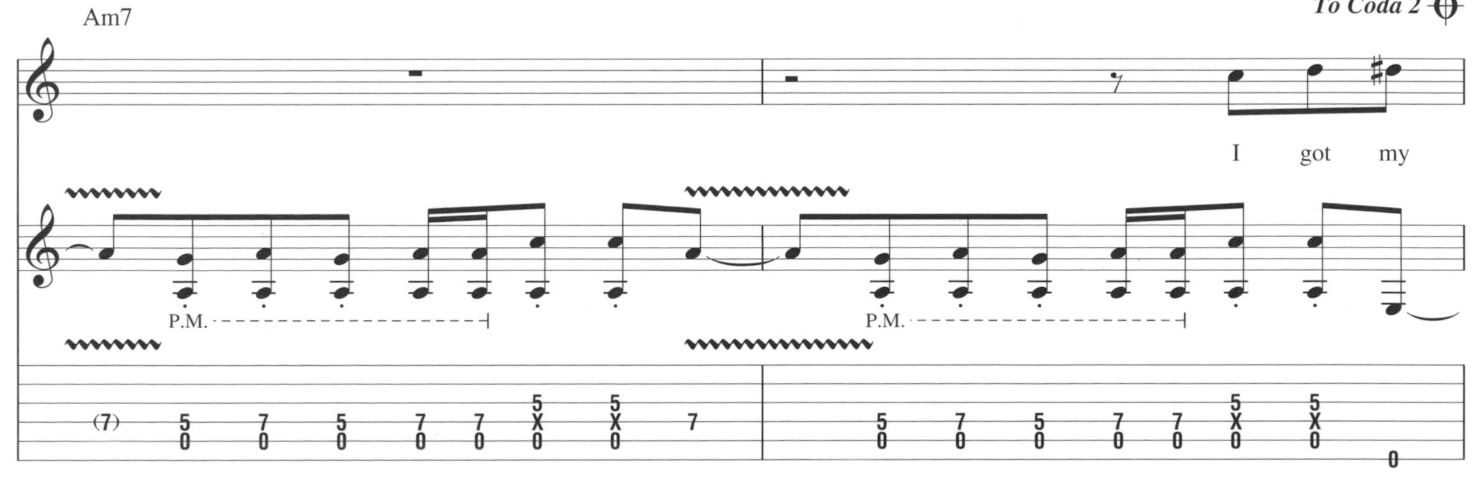
Am7
To Coda 2
I got my
P.M.
P.M.

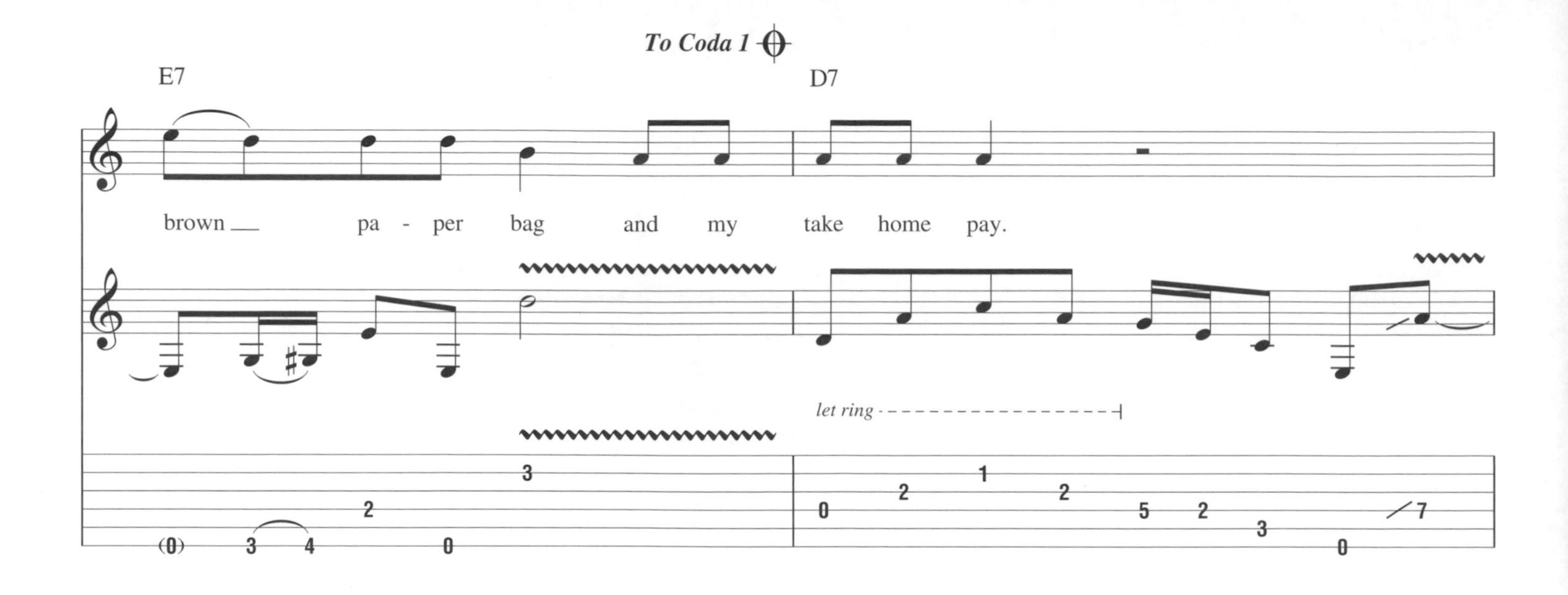
To Coda 1
E7
D7
brown ___ pa - per bag and my take home pay.
let ring
3
2 1 2
0 2 5 2 7
(0) 3 4 0 3 0

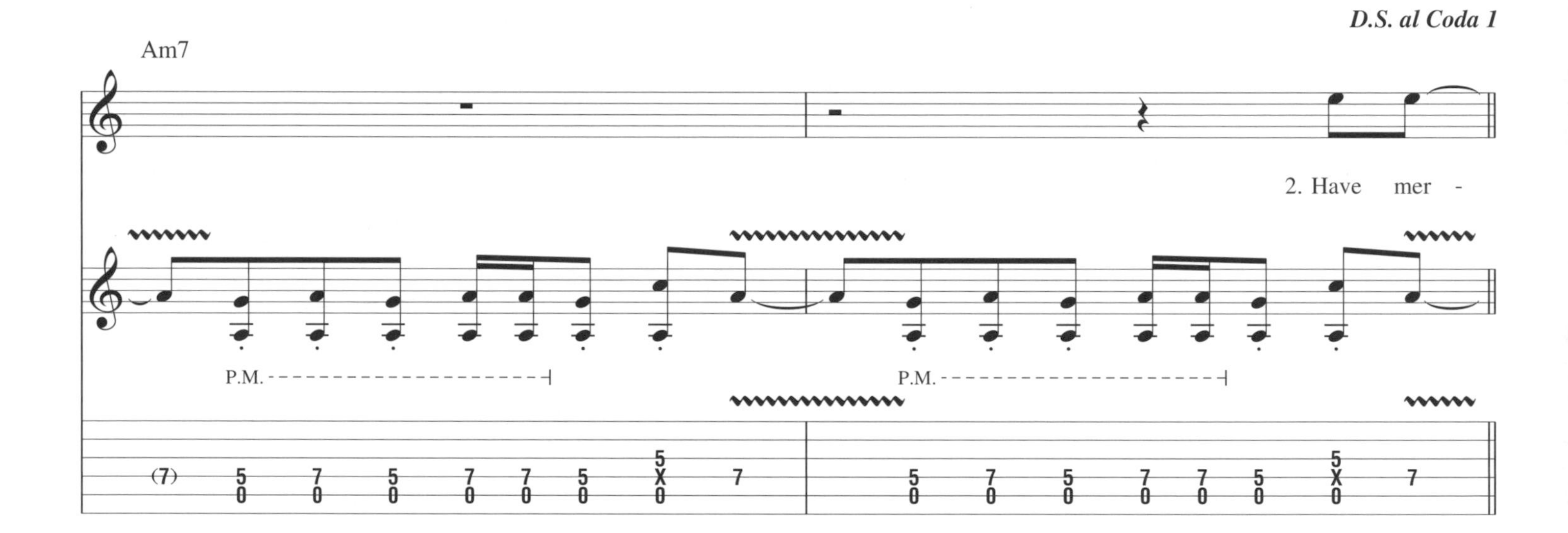
D.S. al Coda 1
Am7
2. Have mer -
P.M.
P.M.
5 5
(7) 5 7 5 7 7 5 X 7 5 7 5 7 7 5 X 7
0 0 0 0 0 0 0 0 0 0 0 0 0 0

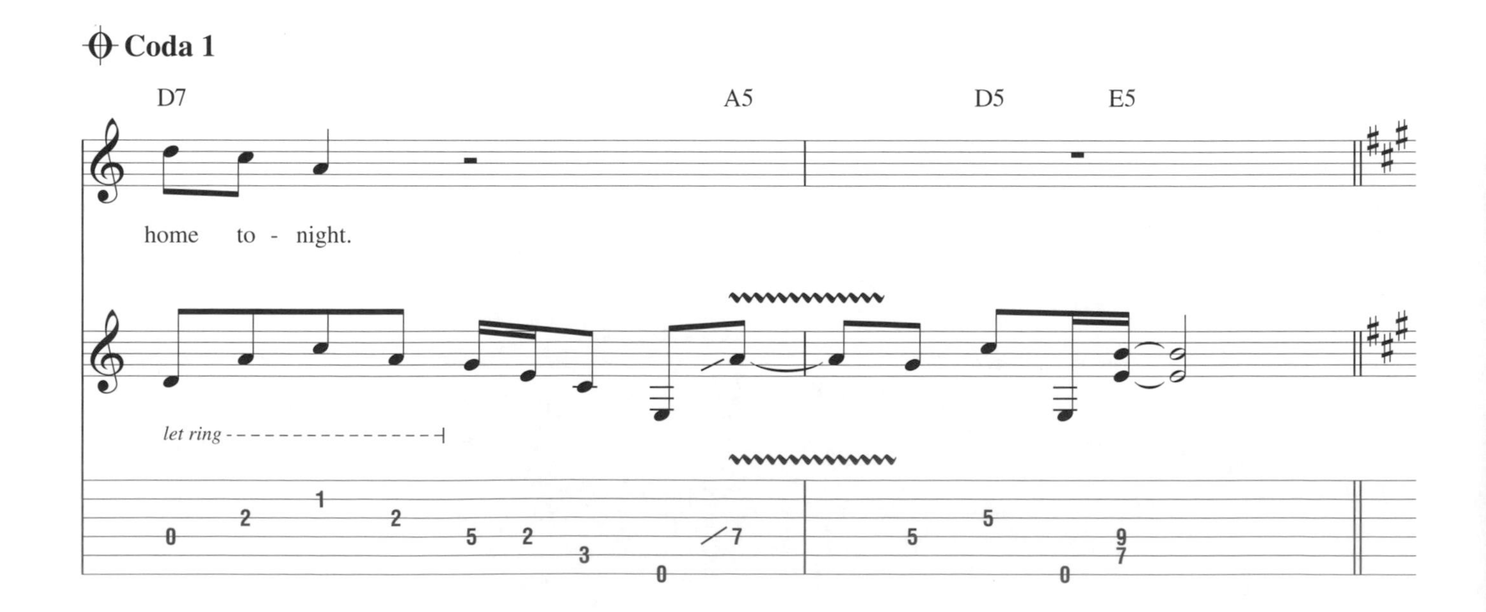
Coda 1
D7
A5
D5
E5
home to - night.
let ring
1
2 2 5
0 5 2 7 5 9
3 0 7
0

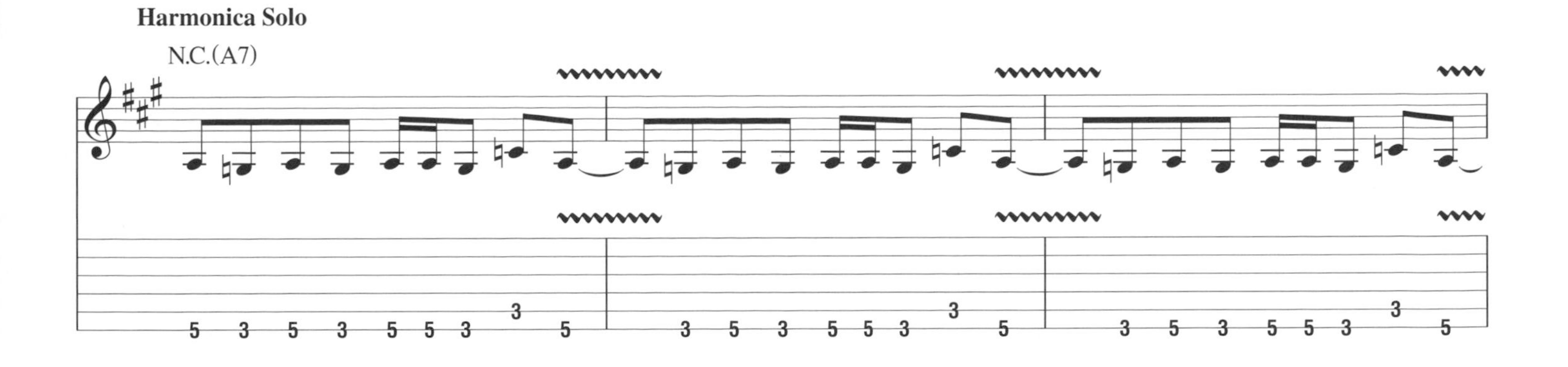
Harmonica Solo
N.C.(A7)

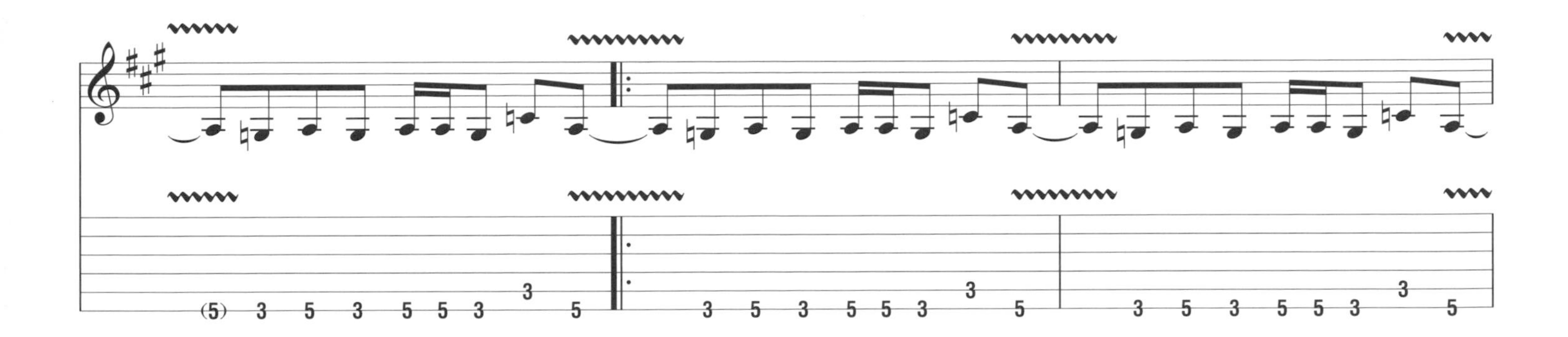

1.
2.

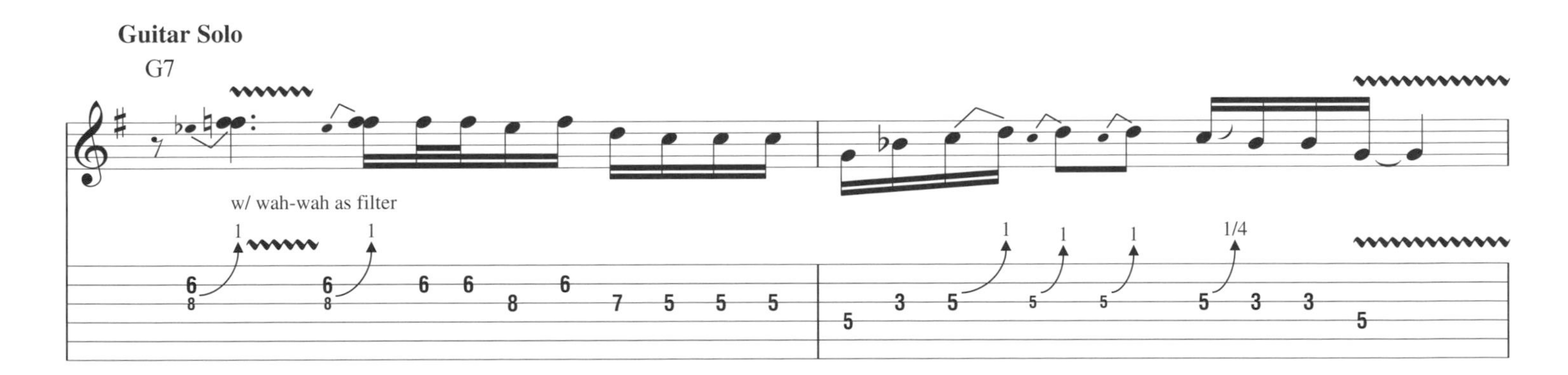
Guitar Solo
G7
w/ wah-wah as filter

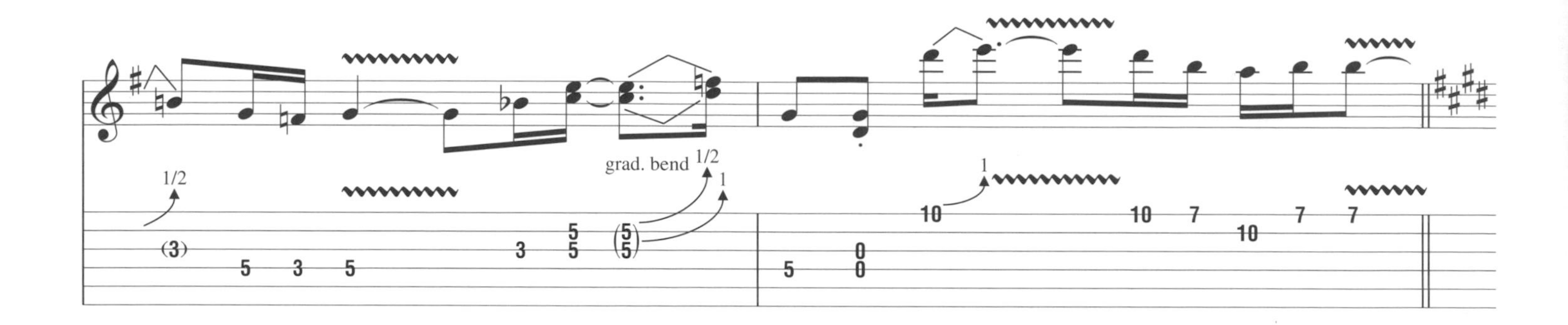

Interlude

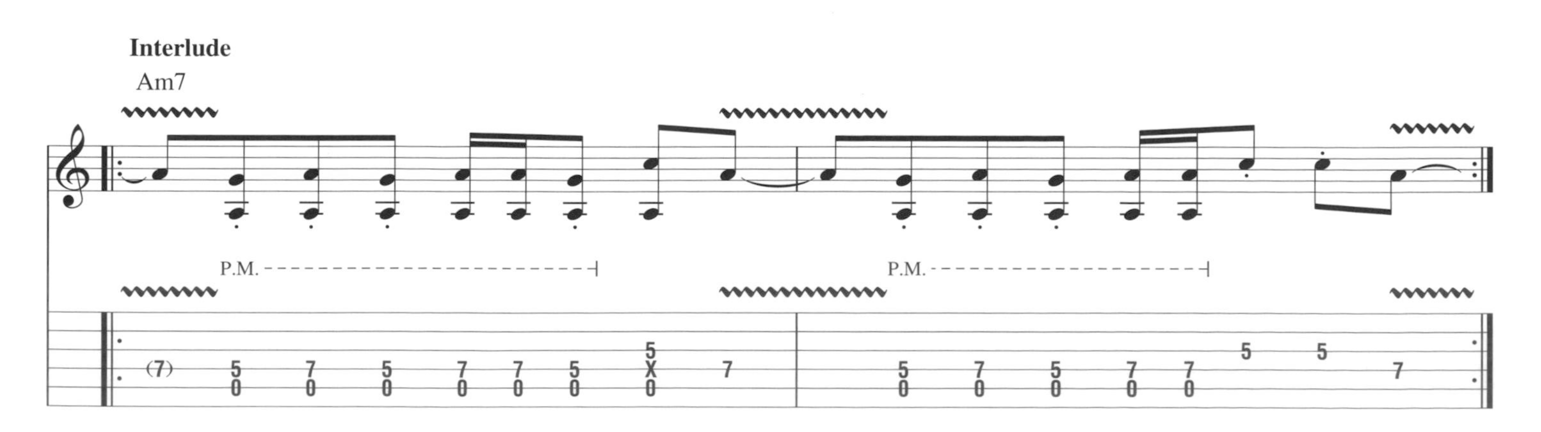

D.S. al Coda 2

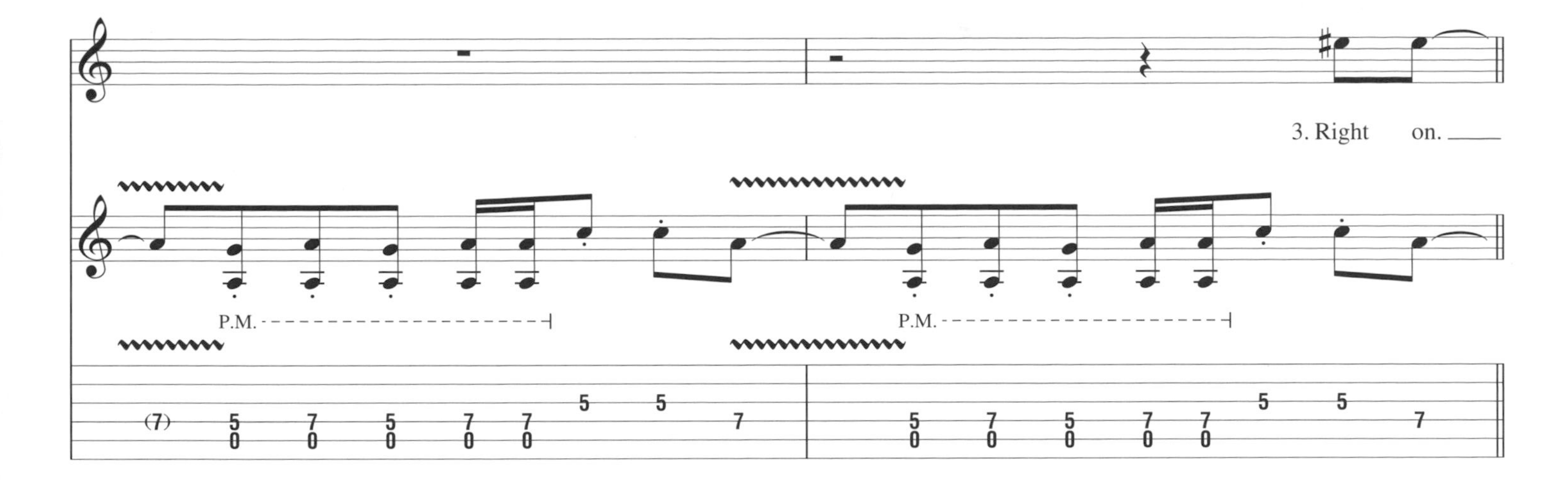

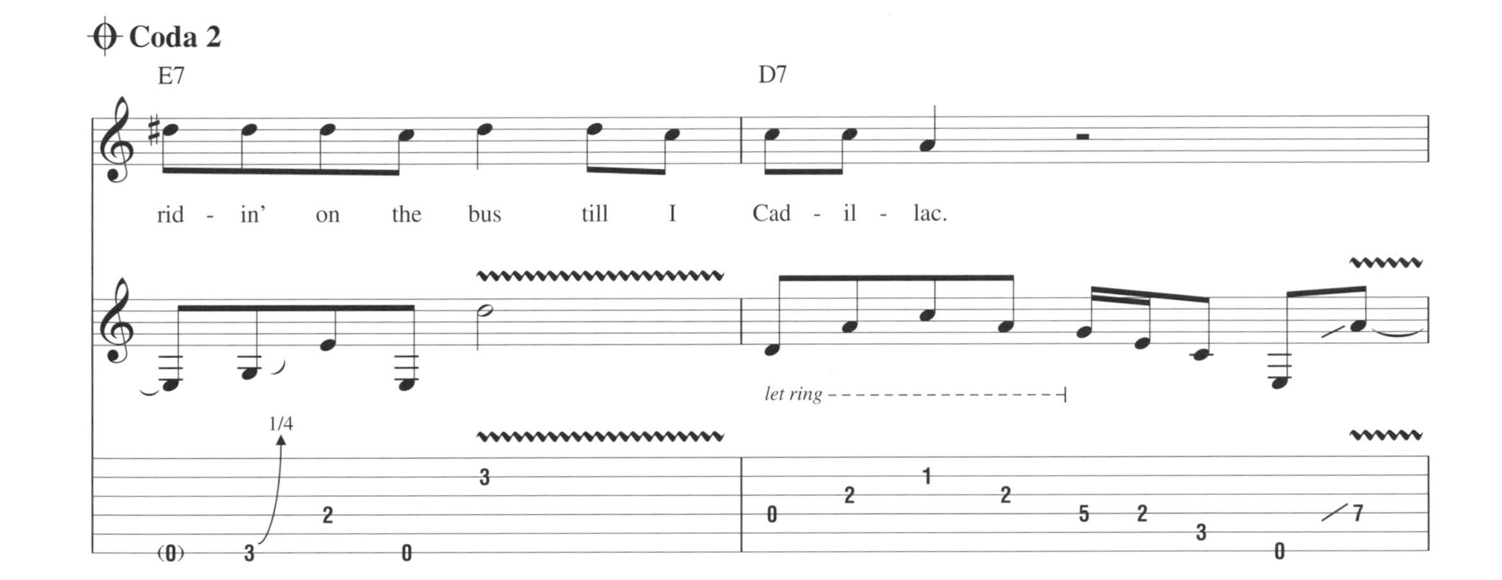

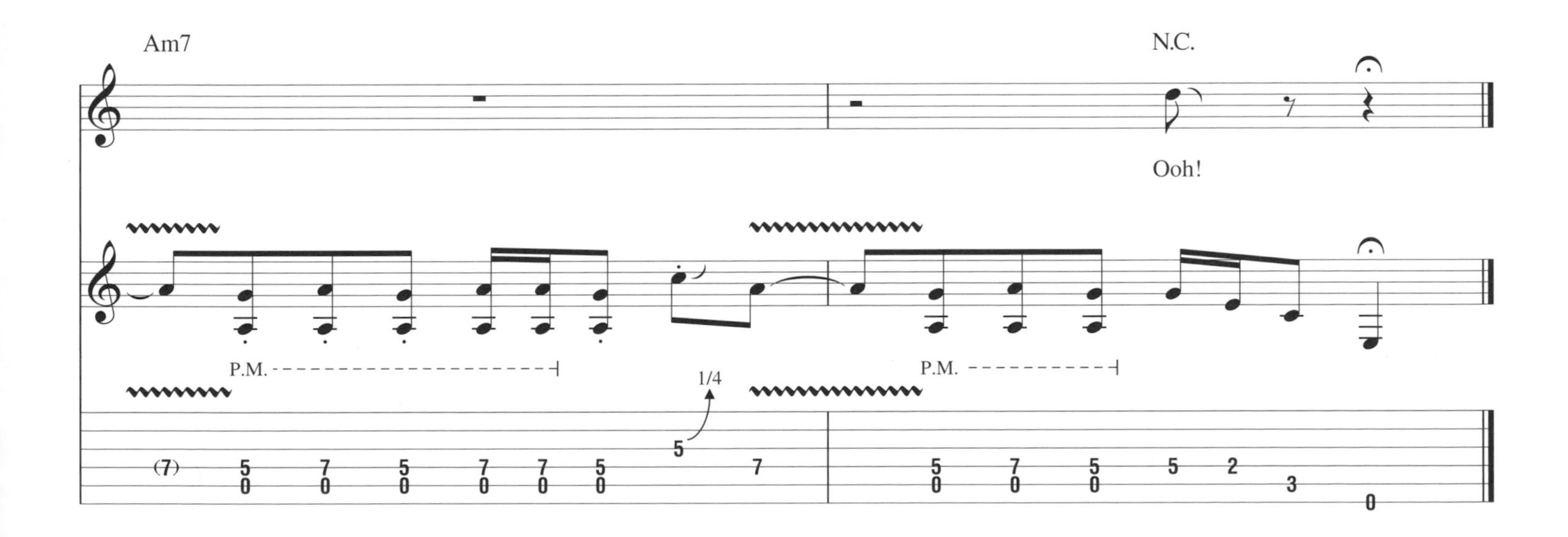

Additional Lyrics

2. Have mercy.
   Ooh, old bus be packed up tight.
   Have mercy.
   Old bus be packed up tight.
   Well, I'm glad just to get on and get home tonight.

3. Right on.
   Ooh, that bus done got me back.
   Right on.
   That bus done got me back.
   Well, I'll be ridin' on the bus till I Cadillac.

Tush

Words and Music by Billy F Gibbons, Dusty Hill and Frank Beard

C7
N.C.
I ain't ask - in' for much.
P.M.
G7
D7
Mm.
I said, Lord, take me down - town.
To Coda
1.
C7
G7
C5 C♯5 D5
I'm just look - in' for some tush.
2. I've been bad,
2.
G7
C5 C♯5 D5
Yeah.
w/ slide

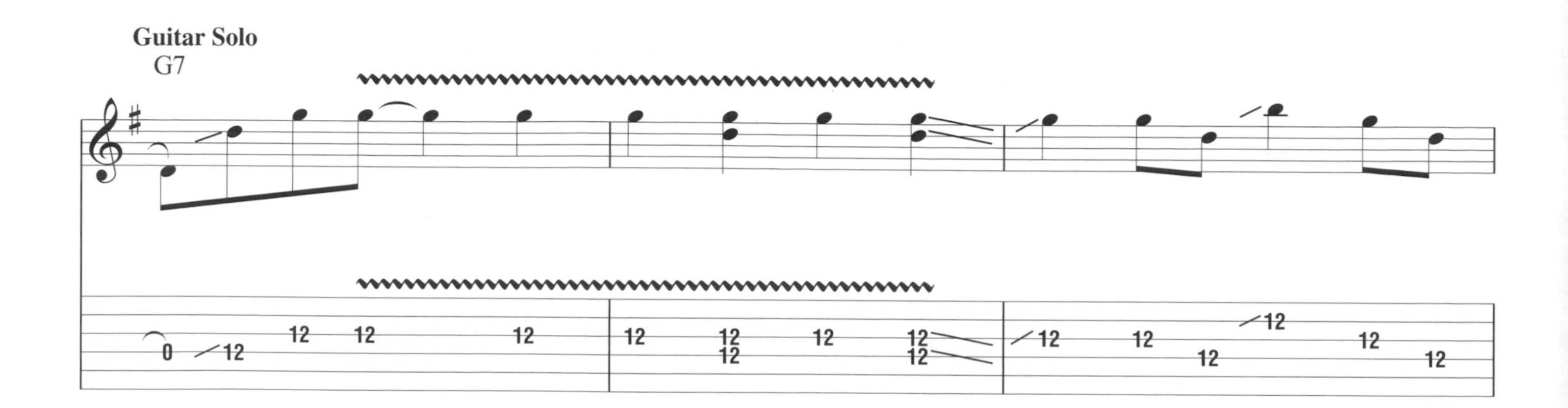
Guitar Solo
G7

G♯5
A5
B♭5
C7
N.C.

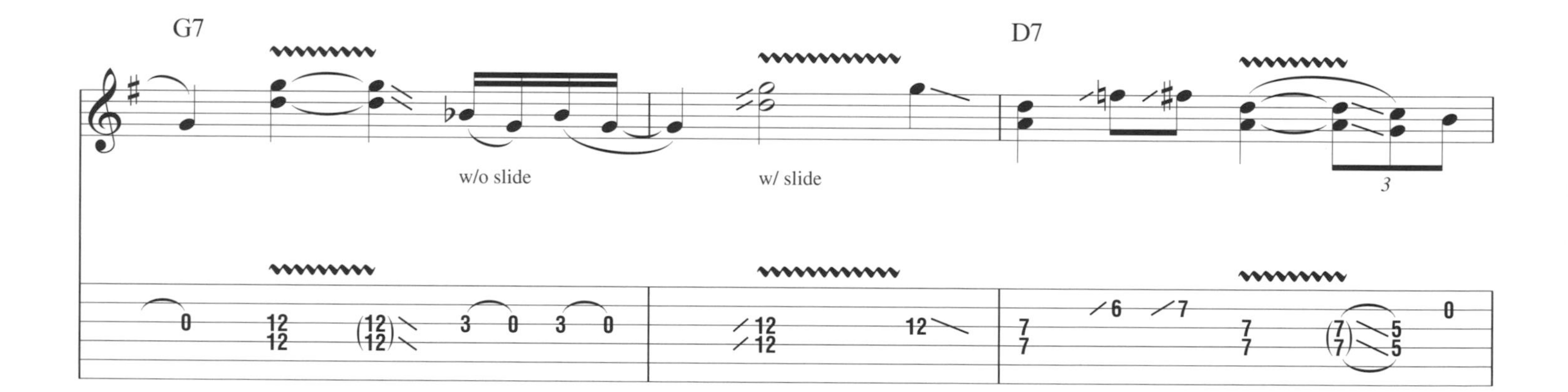
G7
D7
w/o slide
w/ slide

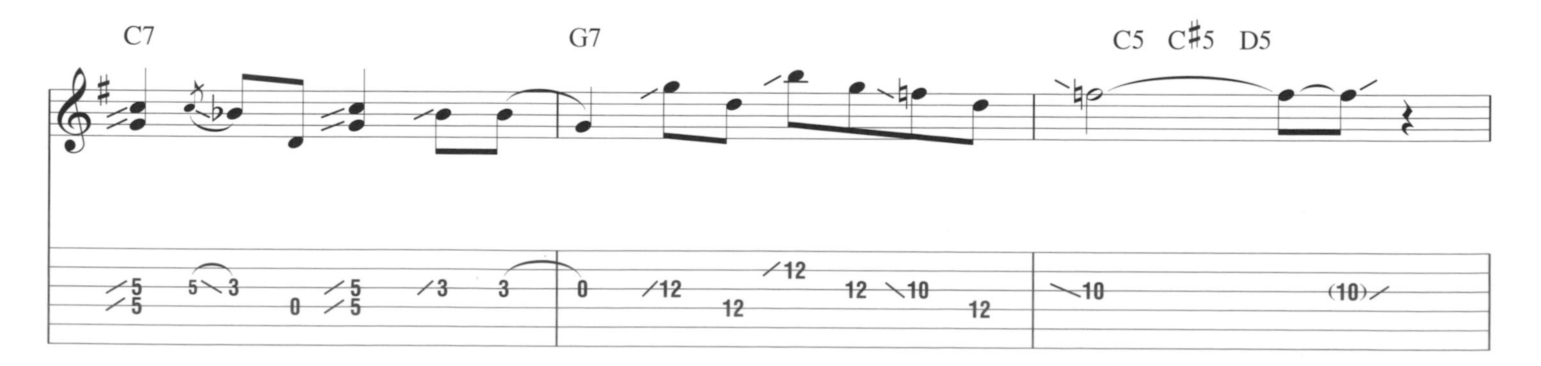
C7
G7
C5
C♯5
D5

G7
G♯5
A5
B♭5
let ring

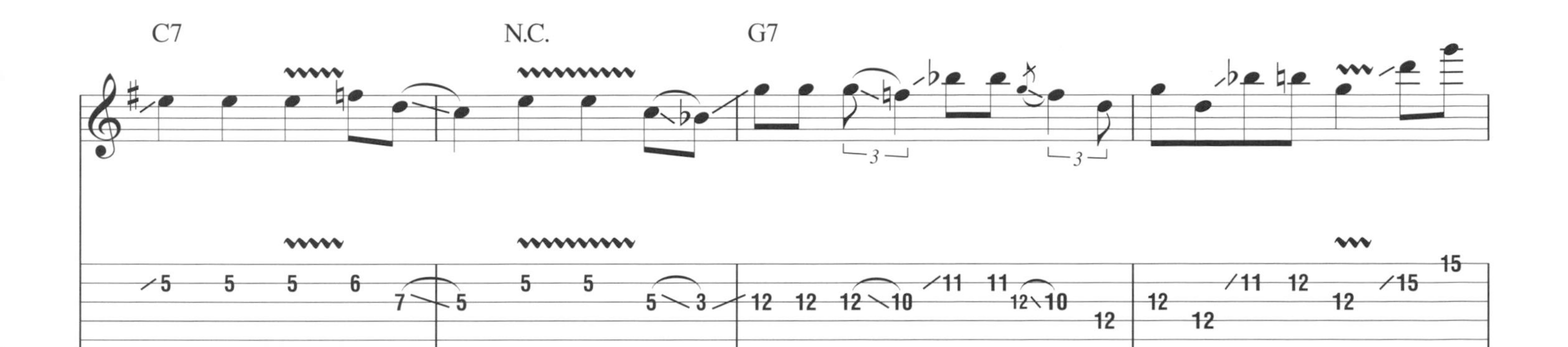

C7
N.C.
G7

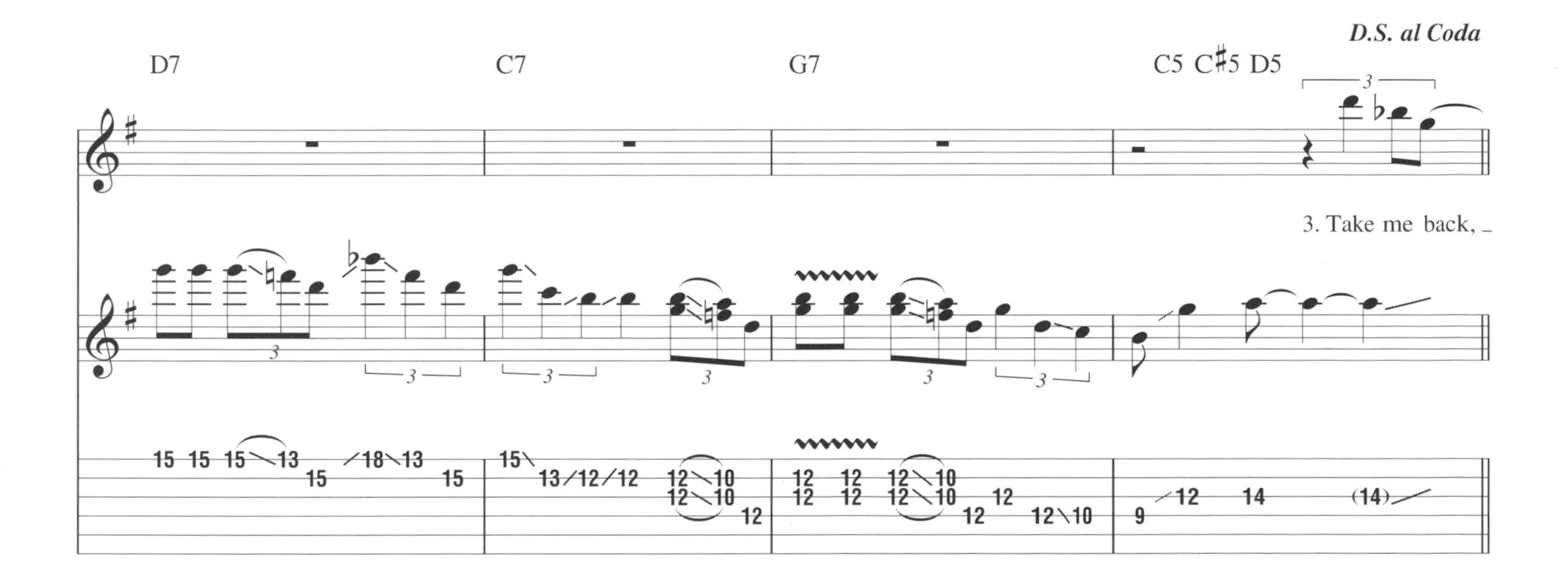

D.S. al Coda
D7
C7
G7
C5 C♯5 D5
3. Take me back,

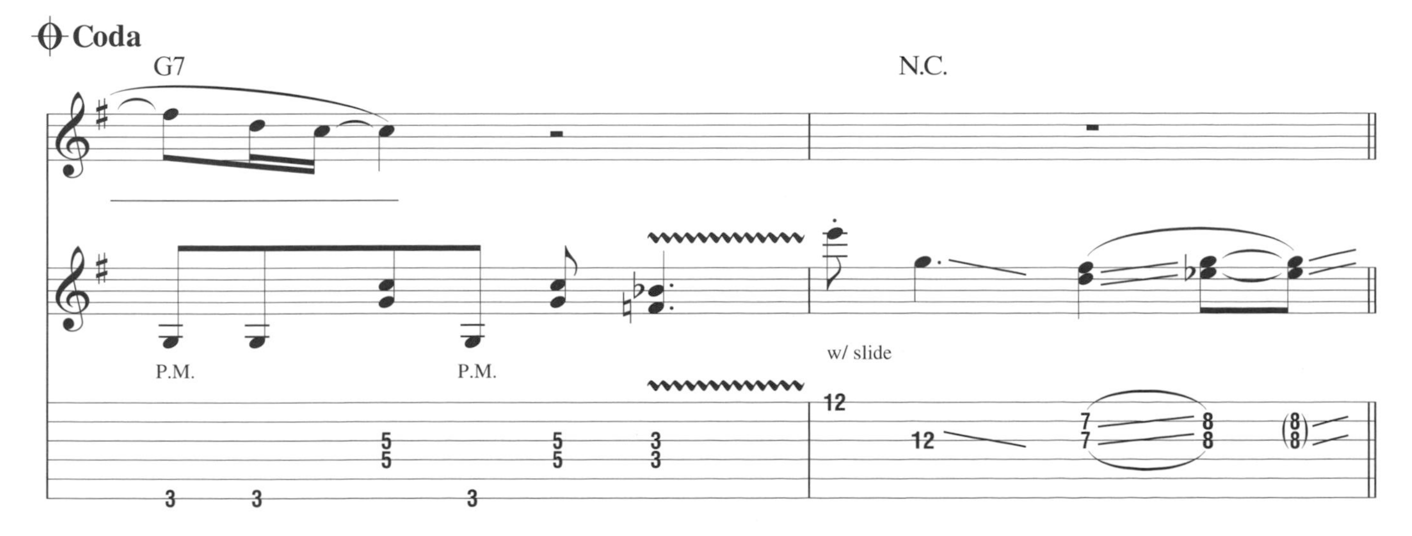

Coda
G7
N.C.
P.M.
P.M.
w/ slide

Outro-Guitar Solo

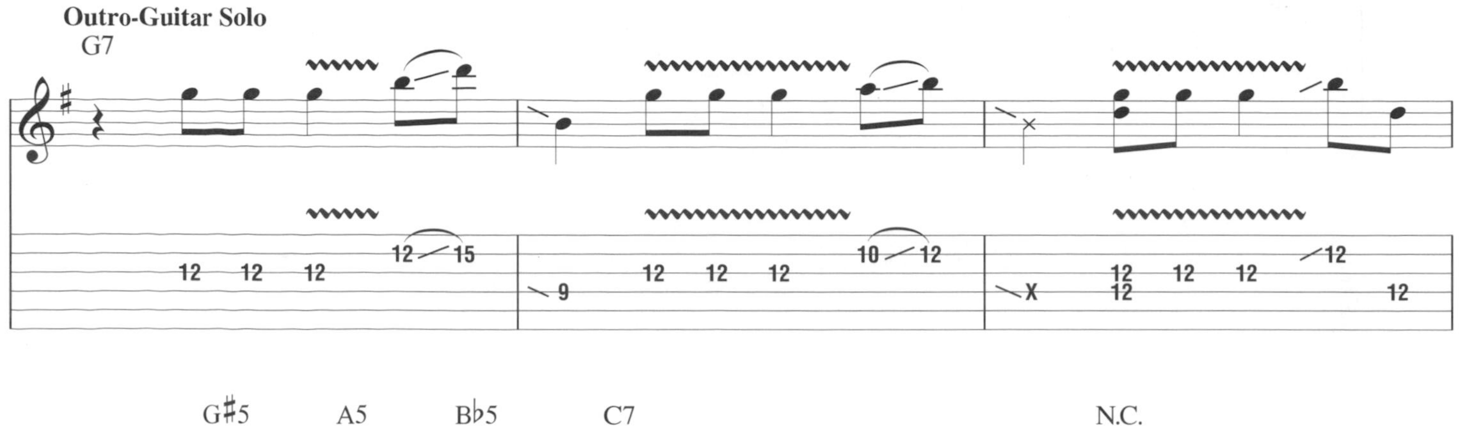

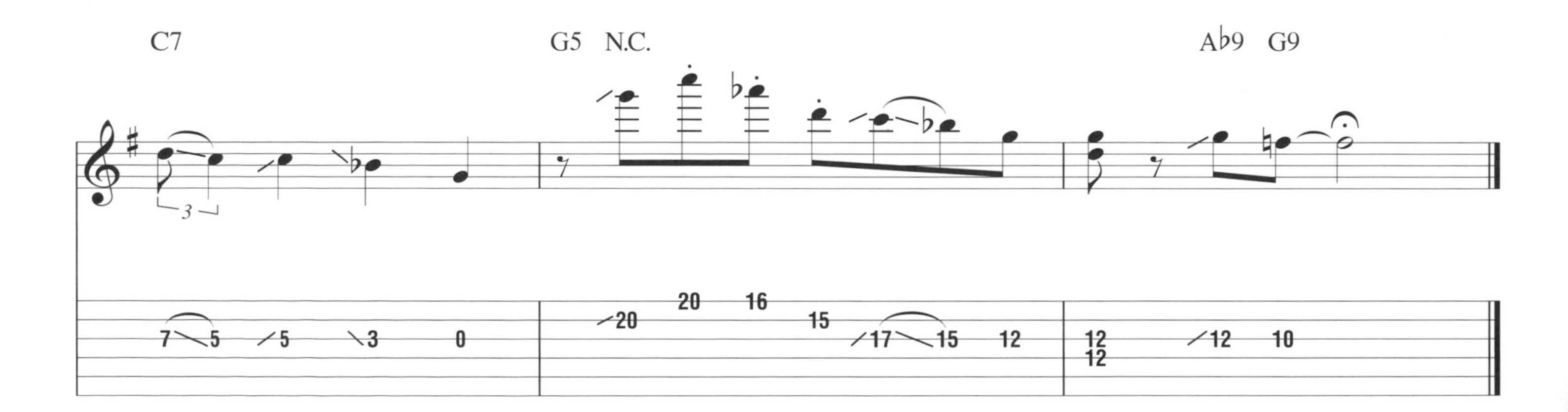

Additional Lyrics

2. I've been bad, I've been good,
   Dallas, Texas, Hollywood.
   I ain't askin' for much. Mm.
   I said, Lord, take me downtown.
   I'm just lookin' for some tush.

3. Take me back, way back home,
   Not by myself, not alone.
   I ain't askin' for much. Mm.
   I said, Lord, take me downtown.
   I'm just lookin' for some tush.